This Love Within

Shira Bliss

...an inspirational memoir
with a lyrical flow and self-help twist!

ISBN: 979-8-9856146-0-2 (Paperback)
ISBN: 979-8-9856146-1-9 (Electronic Book Text)

Front cover image courtesy of Dreamstime.
Book design by Lilly Penhall

Images throughout the book are courtesy of Shutterstock, except for image on page 150 courtesy of Dreamstime, and images on pages 72, 83, and 199 illustrated by Cindy Blaser.

Printed in the United States of America.

First printing edition August 2022.

Bliss House Publishing
San Diego, California

www.shirabliss.com

Praise for Shira Bliss

I have known Shira for many years and have personally watched her transformational journey. In This Love Within, *follow her on this journey through her lyrical words. If you like poetry with a self-help twist, then this is the book for you.*

— **Kevin Anthony**, men's coach and co-host of The Love Lab Podcast

Dear Shira Bliss, Singing Poetess: Thank you for your magic and your healing. Thank you for singing your poems to me. Your voice is pure and natural. I find your songs to be very healing. You're one of a kind and you know how to love unconditionally. Congratulations on your book; I can feel your heart in it.

— **Kathleen O'Brien**, singing coach and former president, National Association of Teachers of Singing (San Diego chapter)

Shira's not your typical British lady with the stiff upper lip. Although she does have a serious side, the innocent girl in her often comes out to play. Take a break, pour a cup of tea, and cozy up with her book of poetry; you won't be sorry.

— **Dave Markowitz**, best-selling author and medical intuitive

More Praise for Shira Bliss

Even if you're not one to typically read poetry, do yourself a favor and read Shira's insightful healing journey. For those of us who tend to judge ourselves harshly, Ms. Bliss' poems will captivate and transform you to a place of self-love and acceptance. If you suffer from overthinking, depression or anxiety, you've come to the right place for help with this grand peak into Shira's big beautiful heart.

— **Dr. Lauren E. Pichard, PsyD,** CEO Ascension Psychology, Inc.

It is my privilege to know Shira! She has a balanced mix of loving herself and giving to others. I have observed that she is always there with a listening ear and you can count on her to help with her practical words of wisdom. I'm thrilled that her book is out so others can be inspired to live a life full of love and bliss.

— **Angeline M. Hart**, best selling author, relationship coach, keynote speaker, and co-founder of Gorilla Love

Contents

Preface xiii

Author's Note xiv

My Journey xv

How to Use This Book.................................xvii

Section 1: The Pain...................................1

Richter Scale 2

Static Quo.. 3

Wistful 4

The Same.. 5

If The Glove Fits.. 6

Where Are You?... 8

Posthaste.. 9

Acting Like My Lover 10

Brass Ring 12

Fortified 13

Wriggly 14

Hey You..16

Parched..18

Becoming Friends.......................................19

Graceful.. 20

Pain & Rebirth..21

the genuine article.....................................24

Skin and Funny Bones................................25

Comfort Or Pain? 26

Rise and Fall..27

Wherein I Wander......................................28

Self-Care..29

let it go.. 30

Seven Days (One Weak)..31

let me out..32

Is There Anyone Out There? 33

Ego Speaks... 34

Slow Down...35

Opportunities Knock (Hard!)...............................36

The Performance..37

wish upon a flower 38

Grow Up!..39

The Queen's Road... 40

Section 2: The Process 41

Within Your Smile (Daddy's Home) 42

The Diamond I am Today 44

Ebb & Flow 45

Let It Out... 46

No Waste...47

Where Are My Marbles? 48

Upside-Down... 49

Operation Peace... 50

The Portal...51

Windows of the Heart...52

Sacred Geometry 53

The Designer... 54

Sweet Caramel 55

Embraced..56

unfettered 57

One Step at a Time..58

I Am That..59

Success 60

Stalemate 61

Catharsis..62

Passion Fruit (The Juice of Life) 63

My World 64

Found Treasure 66

Much Ado About Nothing 67

Why Fight? 68

Why Wait? 69

À la carte 70

Pizza Delivery 71

sanity 72

Groovy Baby 73

The Gift 74

K.I.S.S. (Keep It Simple Sweetie) 75

Face Value...76

Easy Peasy (Shine On) 77

Ego She Go..78

mindless..79

Mindless Too.. 80

Hobnob With Me 81

Balancing Act 82

Unattached... 84

The Way of Flow 85

Giggles & Guffaws.................................... 86

No Vex Flex 87

Silence is Golden......................................88

The Tapestry of Life 89

Loosey-Goosey 90

The Perfect Outfit......................................91

Make Your Mark 92

Do Unto Others..93

To Err is Human.. 94

Momentum...95

What If... 96

More 97

Non-Toxic 98

Hurry Slowly... 99

Rise Above... 100

Self-Absorbed or Self-Love..............................101

Directions 102

My Companions (Sit Inside Your Being) 103

Counterpoise (Tea and Sympathy) 104

Many Paths — Same Sky 105

The Gentle Gardener 106

Topsy-Turvy 107

Mainstay..108

The Voices in My Head....................................109

Patience 110

Of Love and War (Coming Home)....................111

The "Right" Path (The Way) 112

yin and yang...113

Fails With Flying Colors.................................. 114

Kindling (Earth Angel) 115

Twenty-twenty 116

Calm Rapids 117

Laissez-Faire 118

Get Lost! 119

The City of Wonder... 120

Let Go...121

let go even more 122

Celebrate You 123

Carpe Diem..124

Sans Souci..125

wheat and chaff...126

It Is Enough 127

Nonsense (The Place to Be) 128

Moonlight Kisses 129

Loving What Is 132

"Stand At Ease" 133

The Future of Now...134

Dilly-Dally...135

Nichey Glitchy 136

Sticks and Stones..137

a moment in time..138

Goldilocks 139

Bit By Bit (One Bite at a Time) 140

Section 3: The Promise....................................141

Love Song (To The Beloved Within)...............142

Sailing 143

No Place Like Home (Lush and Lively)...........144

Damn Good 145

Damage and Reparation 146

No Sweeter Sound...147

The Whole Gamut...148

Who Am I?..149

This Love Within..150

Flow...152

Pure Gold 153

Soliloquy..154

Step Inside (A Thousand Kisses) 155

Kinship...156

Unity..157

The Warmth of You 158

I Ride on Your Words..159

First Kiss 160

speechless...161

The Sense of Bliss...................................162

Spot-On!...164

The Forest of Knowing.............................165

Enchanté..166

embracing my age....................................167

Organic...168

Innie Outie...170

A to B..171

full days..172

I Am Love..173

Easy (Breakfast in Bed)............................174

Winds of Change (Reassurance on a
Blustery Day)...175

Let Them Be..176

Hunky-Dory...177

A Pleasant Pause......................................178

Weather Report: Calm with Showers
of Bliss...179

Quiet and Space.......................................180

Perfectly Imperfect...................................181

peachy...182

Happy To Be..183

Love Makes the World Go 'Round............184

Love Affairs...185

Be True to You...186

You are Ideal...187

My Perfect Love..188

Fresh Eyes...190

Timeless..191

Choose You! (The Perfect Date)...............192

cozy and poetry.. 193

Assembled 194

Near & Far 195

Arrived... 196

Arms Open Wide..197

We Are Home 198

Unparalleled 200

warm and golden... 201

True Love.. 202

I've Got You.. 203

Cherished 204

Sit With Me (Lullaby of Friday) 205

Oneness... 206

Full Color... 207

Selfishly Giving... 208

Kismet...209

Self-Talk.. 210

Nowhere Land 211

Heart's Song 212

This Quiet Within 213

First Chakra (Rooted and Grounded)............. 214

The Tryst (Happily-Ever-After) 215

Powered by Twiddle......................................216

The End...217

To Know and Be Known 218

Resources.. 220

Acknowledgements 224

About the Author..225

Alphabetical Index by Title...............................226

*"Can you imagine a place where you
no longer seek love? That place is Within."*
—Shira Bliss.

In *This Love Within*, Ms. Bliss will direct you on a
journey to fully knowing you are loved.

Preface

Does any of this sound familiar?

- Absent or disengaged father

- Looking for love in all the "wrong" places

- Trying to prove yourself / get Daddy (or Mommy) to love you

- Never feeling good enough, that you fit in, or that you matter

If so, this book can help you. In writing it, it has helped me.

Author's Note

It's my wish that pain won't need to be your teacher and that these poems will serve as a mirror reflection of the pure love that you are. May my lyrical poetry inspire, invigorate and encourage you to embrace the blissful life you were born to live.

To enhance your reading experience, you may want to read the poems out loud. This can help you extract the truths.

I have used gender-specific terms such as "she" because I relate to that term. Feel free to use your preferred substitutions. You are also at liberty to substitute my use of "God" with Higher Self, Creator, Totality, Source, Universe...

My Journey

I was born and raised in Belfast, Northern Ireland. My schoolmates were jealous of how pretty I was, so they would regularly beat me up to make me ugly.

I felt ugly inside.

My daddy left me when I was seven years old for another woman. When he divorced my mother I felt abandoned and unloved. I don't remember Daddy ever hugging me. I've been trying to prove I'm lovable ever since.

I've been in a series of abusive relationships. I have five grown children that I homeschooled and raised mostly by myself. I had to keep the children away from their father to protect them. I had my hands full as each child had emotional or physical problems: cancer; blindness; mental breakdowns and incarceration.

We were so poor that the children and I were nourished by handouts from the local food bank. I couldn't even afford to buy them beds. In the winter, when we were sick from the toxic mold in the house, we would huddle together on the floor of the 250 square foot house we lived in.

I experienced panic attacks; I was scared to leave the house. I wanted to die. But, the children needed me.

I'm not sure how I survived, but I did. Now, I'm not just surviving, I'm thriving.

I'm thrilled to tell you I enjoy my own flourishing business that I've had since 2010. At the same time, my best friend became my life partner, and we're still passionately in love to this day.

♥ 💕 ♥

How to Use This Book

Overview

The book has been arranged into three sections: THE PAIN; THE PROCESS; THE PROMISE. The poems can be enjoyed in chronological order or you can open a random page and see what your message is for today.

Do you ask yourself: **Why am I here?**

Perhaps the answer is, we are here:

- **To love and be loved**

- **To enjoy and be enjoyed**

This book will take you on a journey to feeling more love and joy in your life.

What if what you believe isn't true? What if the truth is: You're perfect just the way you are.

I used to look in the mirror and feel hatred towards myself. I felt like a failure. I could never "do" enough to feel good about myself. Now, when I look in the mirror I feel unconditional love and joyful acceptance. **Do you long to feel more LOVE and JOY?** Try the **Self-Reflection Exercises** as you read this book.

SELF-REFLECTION EXERCISES

While you are reading the poems in this book, stressful feelings may arise. When you feel stressed over a present or past situation, here are some questions you can ask yourself:

What am I feeling?

Identify any uncomfortable feelings (e.g. I feel sad, angry, afraid). When you've identified how you feel, ask yourself:

When have I felt that before? When did I first feel that?

If you believe you're not loveable or good enough, you may feel uncomfortable emotions like sadness or anger. Your feelings are valid and have served a purpose to show you what you believe.

Is what I believe true?

Your beliefs drive your feelings. If you can see that your beliefs might not necessarily be true, you can shift how you feel. **Can you imagine how you would feel without that belief?** Your feelings can help you determine what you need. Now, ask yourself:

What do I need?

Identify what you need (e.g. I need reassurance, security, connection).

USEFUL TOOLS

When you identify your feelings and what needs they relate to, you empower yourself to live a full and rewarding life. The two charts, in the **Resources** section at the end of this book, are useful tools to use while reading the poems. When you need help identifying your feelings, use the first chart. The second chart is used to help identify your needs.

Summary

It can be useful to examine any beliefs that are harming us. When we drop harsh judgements of ourselves and others, we can change our beliefs. Realizing we are responsible for how we feel and react enables us to meet more of our needs.

DEDICATION

Dedicated to those who choose love.
Again, and again, and again.

Section 1

The Pain

"I want to curl into a ball,
make this painful world go away."
—Shira Bliss

Do you feel like you can't cope?

When deep in pain it's hard to believe you'll ever feel good again. There seems no way out. You want relief. Once in a while there's a glimmer of hope... and then darkness resumes. You feel like you can't cope, some days you don't even want to try. You desperately wish for better days.

Richter Scale

I'm tired of trying
to stand upright.
A tsunami of tears
is my familiar plight.

I wept tonight...
Sadness has me in its grip.
Depression is my companion
on this melancholic trip.

Watch me as I quickly shift—
elation to deflation.
Basing my peace and happiness
on this and that situation.

This world within that I find
is a landslide of despair.
Heart is aching, no escaping
these aftershocks I bear.

♥ 💕 ❤

Are we turning up the volume of our pain to gain attention? Don't tune into that low frequency. Return to the Self-Love channel.

Static Quo

Crackle, crackle, hiss, hiss...
what shall I say is your bandwidth?

Moving forward
perhaps
or could it be
side to side
to catch my breath
perchance I go
backwards
into oblivion
I wish
for that numbness
that calms my angst.

♥ ❣ ♥

A blank slate is the slate to be.

Wistful

I feel around and nothing is seen,
not even a wisp, not even a dream.
It's as clear as night, as dull as light,
a dusky soul, attempting flight.

My content is empty,
upon this canvas there is plenty.

Hushed is my being
no insight revealing
a blank slate creating
words without meaning.

Upon this void, the truth I must
curl up and sleep until I'm dust.
Or, maybe for a moment I'll rise to the moon
to begin or end, this pretty cocoon.

My content is empty,
upon this canvas there is plenty.

♥ ♥ ♥

The Same

She's unenthused as she walks from room to room,
the same room, after the same room, after the same room.
Expecting to find something bright, something shiny,
something with meaning, something aligning.

This current life is filled with the same,
she's not complaining, it's just a game.
The rooms are filled with grandness,
laughter and tears, celebration and sadness.

Today there's a spark that has remained,
yet there's nowhere to go in this world of the same.
Back then she opened doors and walked to new worlds,
doors that were exposed, bright and unfurled.

Who knows what's out there with all their constrictions
and the restraints we add to the shackles and conditions.
The birds are free as they expand their wings,
in their man-made cages, they are let out for their sins.

The people we see are disguised as puppets;
this ruse we know is a fabricated ruckus.
Are there kindred folk to find,
a chosen clan that's so inclined?

From room to room, I step out and see
the choice of embracing my heart as free.
As I muster up my edges and walls,
I become the designer in charge of what calls.

♥ ❣ ❤

I look to men to fill my empty places. The fix is temporary — like an addict who can't get enough.

If The Glove Fits

You think it is I who's being the tease,
counting on me for you to please.
In the end you weren't satiated,
blaming me, yet you initiated.

Perhaps yes, I'm a bit of a vixen,
my world is warm and decidedly golden.
Bliss is the dance that shines from my eyes
as worlds of others move and collide.

You look at me with your cocky stare,
proceed to lay me down and bare.
Don't deny falling in love a little,
exposing your guise of noncommittal.

*I cry as I've been taken
to a place that is mistaken
with someone I want to know.*

The design of you is not my style,
yet I'll play this fiddle a while.
You thought that you could not be fooled,
that you would make and bend the rules.

You played the gigolo, I knew all along,
kept watch on my heart so as not to be laid upon.
You bid me farewell in your sarcastic tone,
and I find once again I'm on my own.

I cry as I've been taken
to a place that is mistaken
with someone I want to know.

♥ ♥ ♥

Where Are You?

What is Father?
To me a nonentity—
a decided gap
in my identity.

Where is the man
who can take the place
and step into the role
of a heart laid waste?

♥ 💕 ❤

There are no pointless feelings. Can you be brave and let yourself feel them all?

Posthaste

I don't want to feel,
it hurts so deeply.
I'll close my heart
and curl up completely.

A life devoid of passion is dry,
a moment without feeling is a waste.
A closed heart is not living at all,
I'll take my chances posthaste.

♥ ♥ ♥

The cynical me trusts only one thing...

Acting Like My Lover

Who are you
acting like my lover?
One moment you're with me,
the next with another.

I called you, "friend"
you numbed my pain,
yet you were limited,
your shelf-life did wane.

I embraced your moods,
you were predictable,
a trusted friend,
you became irresistible.

Now you're gone,
look what you did to me,
a wanton woman
with only myself for company.

I was almost full
yet not satiated,
a tease you are,
once loved, now hated.

I drank you in
the fine wine aplenty,
every crevice you filled,
every crevice you emptied.

Why am I lacking
when all of you is mine?
You're not enough,
I'm leaving you behind.

For God's sake,
I'll not wither on the vine.
I'm moving on,
not wasting my time.

I'll wake up again,
empty, full or resigned.
Wanting nothing, wanting all—
another bottle of wine.

♥ ♥ ♥

Brass Ring

With sunken eyes, she peers through the bars.
The warden shuffles the discharge papers.
The key glimmers, just out of reach
adding to the piteous torment.

She paces back and forth
a deeper groove into the trench of her cell.
The taste of freedom teases her lips
as her monomaniacal mantra is released:
Open the damn door!

♥ ❥ ♥

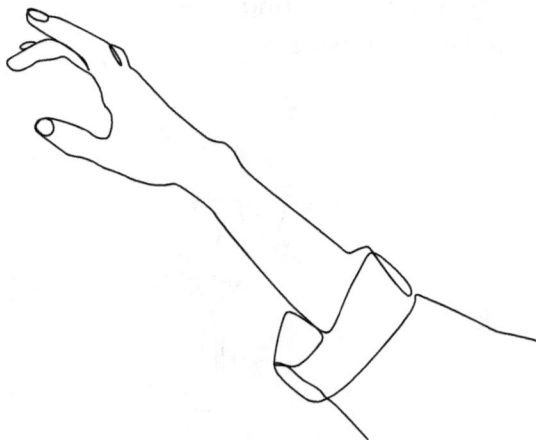

Fortified

So tired, can't decide
whether to sit or stand.
Lacking gumption, how to function
and spice up feelings of bland.
Another day, going my way,
won't you take my hand?
Guide me through, to the heart of you
fortified to withstand.

♥ ❥ ❤

Can you extend that same compassion you give to others to yourself?

Wriggly

What do you do
when the bottle is empty,
the climax complete
and there's no longer plenty?

What do you do with no energy to walk,
what do you do with no words to talk?
Do you wander, looking for connection,
do you wallow in deep dejection?

Why, I ask, is it so hard to find
a friend, a partner with vibration of kind?
A loving, kindred soul who's true,
harmonious and gracious, compatible with you.

Familiar or new, it's all a wash,
a bottomless hole from where I watch
this quiet din I cannot see,
the presence directly in front of me.

I do belong in this heart of mine,
where all is sweet and all is fine,
yet to wriggle, writhe, peek through the veil
is a wholly undoing, delightful tale.

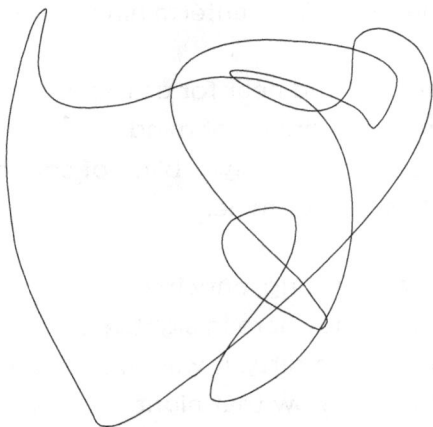

♥ 💕 ♥

Hey You

Did I state my story
(the poems upon my bed)
of broken love that was mended
with needle and a thread?

Hey you... I'm awake,
the door is ajar.
Lines of people are clamoring
for dreams from afar.

They want to hear from you and me,
I must not keep them waiting.
I turned around and didn't see
your One-Man-Show entertaining.

I searched far and near for us to be
featured in this dream of mind.
I looked around with eyes blind of sound
to play this part of mine.

Our fans are waiting, anticipating,
yet you were nowhere in sight.
So, I sang a little ditty, it was ever so pretty—
I hoped you'd show that night.

Hey you... I want you here,
they've begun to arrive in scores.
To celebrate endings and chart our misgivings,
they're lining up for more.

Upon my own (as you were not home),
I donned all the magic I could find.
Went knocking on doors, trading jobs for chores
until I was out of rhyme.

I long to tell you the life of my story,
I turned over, and you were not there.
I searched under cover, from here to out yonder,
but you had forgotten to care.

I tell you they're ready, I'll hold them steady,
they're waiting for us, don't you know?
I look around, you can't be found,
so on stage by myself I must go.

Hey you...
I'm certain you're there,
or why would I talk
to nothing but air?

Listen now (I'll take that bow),
all I need is you.
Say goodbye to the crowds,
close our doors (it's so loud),
and pull up a chair for two.

♥ ♥ ♥

Do you feel like no one gets you?

Parched

I'm desert dry,
rain is welcome.
No words to try,
no one to claim them.

♥ 💕 ❤

Becoming Friends

Pain tries to become my friend—
I told her no. You are not my friend.

Even when I close the door
she has one foot in the way.

Today I opened the door
and invited her in.

"I will be your friend," I said.
And together we sat and had tea.

♥ ❥ ♥

Graceful

Why is it that
many need pain
to awaken to an existence
without suffering or constraint?

I've had so much,
pain that is,
that I'm ready to gracefully
grow and live.

♥ 💕 ❤

Sometimes we have questions, and the Universe is silent, and that's OK.

Pain & Rebirth

I soften and I open
even more—
and rest
as I let it be.
Amidst pain, soften for ease,
soften for acceptance and peace.

I weave my way
into the middle,
I lie there with arms open wide.
Lying flat
exposed
letting pain cover me inside.

Engulfing me inside and out,
watching, listening, open.
Prevailing
Powerful
Pain
Completely complete and broken.

At night the pain
was mighty strong,
I would scream
and then I'd laugh.
Laugh at the ridiculous intensity,
the hope that this can't last.

Feeling and growing,
cocooned
and then a moth.
Expanding this vessel
to overflowing—
more joy, more love, no loss.

I have a new skin
like a snake that's shed
to be wider, deeper and filled.
I've been alone
through all of this—
The Beloved In Me fulfilled.

At times I'm afraid,
then I remember:
Trust is the place to be.
When the pain gets so high
that I'm in fear of my life,
I breathe deeply into my belly.

All I can do is breathe,
more deeply than before, yet
each
breath
hurts
as I expand my belly for more.

I cry to the angel of mercy for help,
I cry to the angel of healing.
I get no answer,
it's all a void,
nothing clear
is revealing.

To birth something new
I must allow
the shedding of skin
for transformation.
Everything is as it needs to be—
this is my salvation.

♥ ❣ ♥

"Will the real you please stand up?"

the genuine article

a worse tragedy
than death would be
if i lived to my end
a false copy of me

♥ ❣ ❤

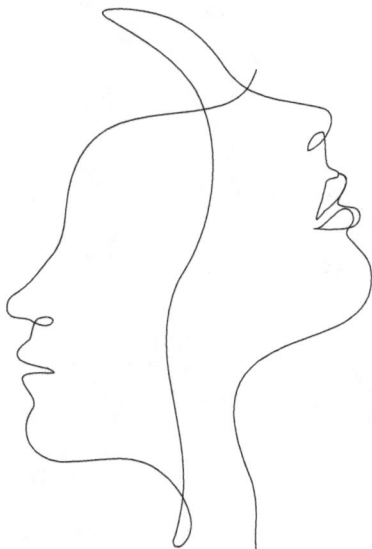

Skin and Funny Bones

Funny, they say, write something funny;
your poems are so very dour.
Funny, they say, where is your wit?
Your poetry's flat and sour.

I can't incite a giggle,
not a single line of mirth.
I've attempted to amuse,
I've tried for all I'm worth.

Perhaps my wit is sleeping,
I've tucked her deep in bed.
The jokes have gone for coffee,
it's solemn in my head.

♥ ♥♥ ♥

Suffering is a dis-ease (we get to choose to suffer, or not). Acceptance is the antidote.

Comfort Or Pain?

It's easier to breathe
when you're quiet.
Yet when you shout, I listen.
You're loud and rude,
I don't need you to grow—
it's time to choose my position.

♥ ❣ ♥

Rise and Fall

I build myself up, a wall of bricks—
seemingly strong...

They remove one brick at a time,
just enough to leave you with holes
to where you ache.

Taking secrets you told
(when you felt bold)
to use them against you.

Poking holes in your steady stack,
you come crumbling down—
a pile of rubble, no use at all.

And you wonder...
How do you recover from that?

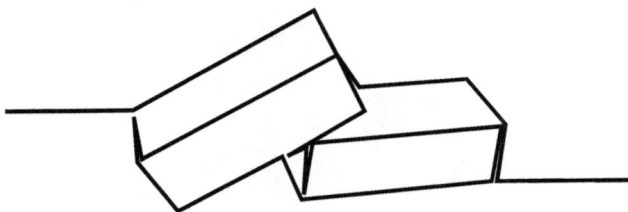

♥ ♥ ♥

Wherein I Wander

In my dream
a bird of prey
landed on my head.
I was afraid
it would carry me off
Where Angels Fear to Tread.

I cried out not knowing
where I was going,
therein my beloved was led
to steer me between
the Devil & the Deep
and tuck me back in bed!

♥ ❥ ♥

Be aware, practice self-care. It's healthy to set boundaries.

Self-Care

Will you set limits and boundaries,
or do you dismiss what you need?
It feels good I know, to avoid conflict and show
how much you love and concede.

Yet, if you leave your joy behind,
only you will suffer the loss.
If you're compromising your pleasures in life
I urge you to take a pause.

It's okay that you accommodate,
yet fully enjoy yourself too.
Even though you delight in giving,
consider what's best for you.

♥ ❣ ♥

let it go

why hold a grudge
refusing to budge
are you the judge

why keep score
that won't get you more
what are you hoping for

♥ ♥ ♥

SEVEN DAYS
(One Weak)

It makes one weak to try
to pass the days we wish would fly
with hope upon our wings.
Gaining strength perchance we'd meet,
at last in long-lost dreams.

♥ 💕 ♥

Are you your own worst enemy?

let me out

within my self-made prison
there is air to breathe
and a smile
begging to be let out

♥ ❣ ♥

Is There Anyone Out There?

Really darling, seriously,
you're bummed 'cause no one's listening?
Haven't I told you
(and reminded you most often)
the only two that matter are you?

♥ ❥ ❤

Ego Speaks

Does it end this discontent,
this "little me" I need to mend?
Will I rest and circumvent
a tormenting mind that won't relent?

I'll take my sleep,
seek oblivion that peaks
upon breathless sighs
as life passes me by.

♥ ♥ ♥

Slow Down

Can I slow down
even more than before,
slow down to observe
what's there to adore?

I'm going to begin
by savoring each bite
of food and darkness
and fragments of light.

♥ 💕 ♥

You can't change the circumstances; however you can change your reaction.

OPPORTUNITIES KNOCK
(Hard!)

Another chance to release and soften,
yes, I'm sick and this happens often.
I'm tired and weary, didn't get a break,
another viral attack—I'm laid out in its wake.

I've been told: Let it flow, let it flow...
it's not easy when pain continues to grow.
I can use this discomfort to be enlightened,
because the alternative's rather frightening.

The truth of the matter is I'm hurting,
why fight this fact that clearly is certain.
An opportunity to practice acceptance could be
to invite more love, more capacity.

♥ ❥ ♥

The Performance

Uplift, downshift,
moving with nowhere to go.
Sitting still, rolling downhill,
searching for nothing I know.

Posing tranquility, feigning virility,
no need to stand so tall.
Walking dead, in my head,
watching the curtains fall.

♥ ❣ ♥

wish upon a flower

you bring me pretty flowers
the cast-offs from your heart
when all i ever wished for
was kindness from the start

♥ 💕 ♥

Grow Up!

Being an adult
is not all it's cracked up to be.
I propose instead,
we play at make-believe.

Would you like to be a Fairy
or perhaps a Beauty Queen?
I'll be a Knight in Shining Armor,
save myself from this silly scene!

♥ ❣ ♥

Practice celebrating yourself as royalty no matter what you, or others, say.

The Queen's Road

How does acting quiet and small
advance my cause, or not at all?
Especially when they add the pressure,
surrounded in pain, I surrender without measure.

Why contract and allow the oppression?
Stand in your worth—no need for aggression.
Be strong, say something or walk away,
take action to keep the insults at bay.

Don't believe the lies you've been told,
that you're incapable, that you need their hold.
It's how they keep you from leaving them,
when you believe you want and need these men.

♥ ❣ ♥

Section 2

The Process

"Everything you feel, see, hear and do is perfect for your highest good—trust that."
—Shira Bliss

Can you feel your feelings fully and accept yourself no matter what?

Suffering is optional. It's our choice. Suffering can become a habit. And, habits can be broken. We can practice letting things go and not allow ourselves to be completely immersed in the suffering.

If we see the pain as temporary (be it physical or emotional), we can use it as a tool for growth and the way to a more comfortable, peaceful life.

We can choose to trust the process.

Can we trust that our parents did the best they could with the tools they had?

WITHIN YOUR SMILE
(Daddy's Home)

I saw your truck
in the driveway today,
my heart skipped a beat,
I'd forgotten you were away.

Daddy's truck's in the driveway
but there's no daddy home.
I'm here once again,
all on my own.

I wish Daddy were here
so we could play,
I wish he were beside me,
to begin this day.

A hole in my heart
I feel is there,
I'm looking for someone,
something to repair.

I can't seem to grasp
what it's like to have the other,
'cuz I've been by myself,
devoid of this lover.

To not have a daddy
is a sad state to be,
so I look to myself
for that masculine entity.

Within my being
is everything I need,
yet those strong arms
I can't seem to concede.

I don't find it inside,
so instead I drop it,
this quest to find him,
the one who calls me "Poppet."

Dear sweetie, dear child,
I love you so much.
Dear daughter, I'm here;
receive my touch.

I know right now you cannot see
the love that's there beaming from me.
Remember my darling, you began from my seed,
my love for you we need not leave.

I'm always here within your heart,
rocking you gently from end to start.
To quiet your noise, have you rest awhile
because my delight is within your smile.

♥ ♥ ♥

This poem is dedicated to the man without whom I would not have become the diamond I am today.

Under the duress of approximately 725,000 pounds per square inch, and at temperatures of 2000 – 2200 degrees Fahrenheit, carbon atoms connect and bond together and a diamond begins to form.

The Diamond I am Today

My heart, a lump of inky coal,
day after day repressed.
Fires of transformation on my own,
yet still I rise oppressed.

Squeezed and smothered, reduced and pressed,
insides turning out.
Not a particularly pleasant feeling
with organs strewn about.

Under duress I began to change,
I saw no other choice.
To succumb or shatter, no longer did matter,
I had given up my poise.

Formed from pressure I became
the gem that's here to stay,
shiny and rich, empowered and free,
the diamond I am today.

♥ ♥ ♥

Up and down I go, on the waves that ebb and flow.

Ebb & Flow

Be still my heart,
you've known greater angst than this.
Yet my soul is spent,
with no drive to exist.

The years are upon me and it shows,
I am only now learning how to grow.

There's a flicker in the clouds,
a warmth within your smile.
My heart speaks volumes of nothingness,
the end of which beguiles.

I hear a cat purr,
a bird's song at my window.
I breathe, I cry, my tears wash me new
as I rise to the next crescendo.

The years are upon me and it shows,
I am only now learning how to grow.

♥ ❣ ♥

Make room for your sorrow and fear, your anger and shame, your joy and gladness.

Let It Out

What to do with un-comfy feelings:
anger, grief, and fear—
acknowledge them, feel them fully,
there's a reason why they're here.

Don't hold them in, let them out,
your body won't thank you to stifle.
Track them back to where they started,
they likely were needed for survival.

♥ ♥ ♥

What would happen if you put off worrying until next Wednesday?

No Waste

Worry was an ingredient
in all the meals I cooked.
Worry was my attitude,
it kept me on its hook.

It added to my image
(the facade I was proud to own)
the consternation of my scowl,
the announcement of my groan.

Only someone who lives forever
has time for worries and fears.
Do I want to waste my moments
on made-up stories and tears?

♥ ❣ ♥

*Be yourself. Nobody else can do you
like you do.*

Where Are My Marbles?

Have you ever had days
you can't find your glasses?
You put on your spare (on top of what's there)
and feel like a herd of asses?

Go easy on yourself
when your mind is hazy.
You've not lost it,
and you're not that crazy.

Your self is intricate, your essence true,
it doesn't change with what you do.
You may have lost your marbles,
but you're still you!

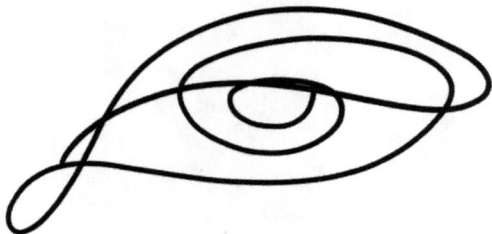

♥ ♥ ♥

Upside-Down

Upside-down, it's the place to be,
unless inside-out is your cup of tea?

My head has taken the space of my feet,
here where creativity can't be beat.

The blood is rushing to my brain,
thus I write this witty refrain.

Upside-down, a great place to be,
where a frown becomes a smile in unique scenery.

Whatever way you look, it is rather silly,
a joker finding herself brazenly dizzy.

Yet, I propose within these words,
you'll find upside-down is your new preferred!

♥ ♥ ♥

When I stop the search, I come face to face with me.

Operation Peace

The search for love,
the search for peace
is what I do
to find release.

Attempting to escape
from my perception of lack,
rejecting "what is"
has become my knack.

When I realize my desire
is for Oneness and Connection,
I can stop the search
and face that direction.

That direction is Me—
no need to look outside,
because within
completeness resides.

♥ ❣ ♥

Pain can be a portal to enlightenment.

The Portal

I used to be an experience junkie,
needing accomplishments to feel successful—
my life was slipping by.

I was asleep.
Now, I'm awake.
Pain woke me; agony was my portal.

I experience the union
between my breath and the air,
the beckoning of trees, a whisper of breeze.

In the marriage of my being, I am one
with the sounds and the silence,
the sights and the darkness...

Upon excavating my soul
I have stepped into a grand canyon
of spacious delight.

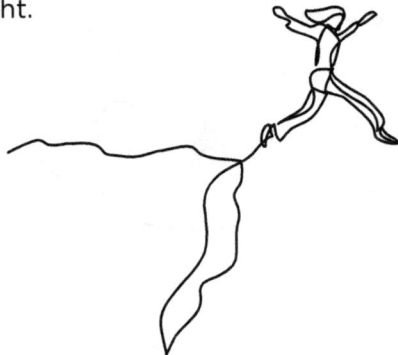

♥ 💕 ♥

Windows of the Heart

You do well to simply breathe
in and out.
Breathe in love,
breathe out fear.

Move your breath in and out,
move it through and through.
Let it harmonize, soothe and stabilize
every part of you.

Your heart has eyes—look from there.
Your heart has limbs—move from there.
Your heart is love,
live from there.

Breathe deeply My Love
in and through your heart.
You do well to simply breathe
in and out.

♥ ❧ ♥

Sacred Geometry

Having expectations
allows room for regrets.
With resentment as my neighbor;
gratitude is bereft.

Why not accept the way
the origami of life unfolds
and capture all the joy
that thankfulness bestows?

♥ ❥ ♥

The Designer

It's raining again,
it stops and it starts
like God has a handle
he turns on and off.

What if I'm God
and I have the ability
to command my sloth
or my agility?

Would you like to adjust
the faucet and see
the flow that would pour,
the weather that could be?

♥ ♥ ♥

Sweet Caramel

Smiling deeply into that which is not visible,
peacefulness takes possession of my heart.
Flowing gently like sweet caramel,
engulfing my end, my middle, my start.

Embracing invisibility fosters ease,
no more chasing significance, no need
to know we matter,
to give all or concede.

No need to go anywhere,
we're already here.
No striving to make a difference,
to maneuver or steer.

Unhindered, gently tethered
to the Pure Love that resounds,
echoing serene choruses,
accepting life's charms.

I acknowledge me,
and that is enough.
My medicine is potent,
and I sip on it as such.

♥ ❣ ♥

Embraced

I took out an ad: "Love Wanted" it read.
"Will work for love," the ad had said.
I was looking for love in all the wrong places,
not knowing how to answer my own love's embraces.

"I don't get you,"
those words don't have to hurt,
what if all that's needed
is to get your own true worth?

♥ 💕 ♥

unfettered

knots have come undone
loose ends are left untied
sleep easily finds me
with nothing on my mind

body lies contented
spirit steps outside
past dusty corners and crevices
unshackled wanton wild

♥ 💕 ♥

That first step is hard. Fake it 'til you make it.

One Step at a Time

When I awaken, I lie in bed
for motivation to move me, yet instead
nothing arises, so I wait some more—
it's a waiting game I'm clearly over.

I'm in the rut of Groundhog Day,
my on/off button doesn't know how to play.
I'm curious for the answer (as I stifle a yawn)
to what would move me to greet the dawn.

Then as I begin to count to five
(before I decide to change my mind)
I'm up and at it, moving about,
one step at a time, no room for doubt.

♥ 💕 ♥

I Am That

I am what I am
no matter what you say.
I am what I am
when my mind says nay.

I am the space between your words,
not the phrases from your throat.
I am the symphonies masters play,
the silence between their notes.

Because we exist, we are of great worth,
no less than the stars, sun, moon or earth.
As valued as oceans, blue skies and streams,
we're beyond perception and even our dreams.

♥ ❣ ❤

I don't make mistakes; I take scenic tours that enrich my journey!

Success

Drop the thoughts of failure,
I encourage you to try.
Don't live your life in fear,
or life will pass you by.

There's nothing to achieve,
you exist, therefore you succeed.
Know that you're enough,
there's nothing more you need.

♥ ❣ ♥

Pay attention, listen to the voice within, wherein resides volumes of quiet wisdom.

Stalemate

It's time, you've reached your limit,
the hands of the clock are paused,
the season to fight has passed,
will you give up and relinquish your cause?

In your self-imposed desert
the clouds have begun to drop,
moisture cools your fevered brow,
you finally yield and stop.

Surrender is the key,
the key to all the doors
to rooms hidden in plain sight
where collections of answers are stored.

♥ ❣ ♥

Catharsis

Cocooned in cotton candy clouds
that soften my brittle bones,
sipping medicine that comes from god
with a side dish of my moans.

I cannot do anything but this,
I need to surrender, not fight.
Resisting hurts me more,
and magnifies my plight.

Feed my bones,
my hurting bones
with medicine from god.

All I can do is loosen
and meet you in the quiet,
nestled in your arms,
sheltered from the riot.

The taste of sweet surrender,
the nectar of your lips to mine.
Tears that belong to no-one,
my cares of life resign.

Feed my bones,
my hurting bones
with medicine from god.

♥ ❣ ♥

When we live our lives with healthy detachment,
we enjoy harmony of mind and body.

PASSION FRUIT
(The Juice of Life)

Shining so bright
stars pale in this light,
amongst facets of dull
and feelings of blight.

A quiet so quiet
it stumbles on dispassion,
this nothingness, this bliss
of inertia in action.

Finding the balance,
if there is such a thing,
where The Juice of Life
still captures my being.

Inside and out,
no need to scrutinize,
when all parts of this whole
echo and harmonize.

♥ ♥ ♥

My World

Look at me
I produced a child
who is thrilling the world.
Look at me
I am just a child.
And I'm thrilling my world.

Look at me
I'm the queen of the hill
I am the snail that is still.
And I'm thrilling my world.

Don't look at me
can't you see
I'm hiding in plain sight.
I am as big as a tree
as busy as a bee.
And I'm thrilling my world.

They've let me out
prison doors open wide
at least enough light
to step inside.
And I'm thrilling my world.

In this audience of one
I plus me equals two
it's not lonely at all
the void is not true.
And I'm thrilling my world.

♥ 💕 ♥

Why wait for that special someone or something
to feel content? Live life fully NOW!

Found Treasure

Inner Peace and I
were truly not acquainted.
She kept herself in hiding,
'til one day she brashly stated:

"The treasure you've been seeking
is hidden in plain sight.
It's not that it's lost and buried;
it's right in front of your eyes."

Why wait for "X" to feel content?
Don't leave fulfillment behind.
Everything you need is already inside;
seek not and you will find.

♥ 💕 ♥

Believe the best, let go of the rest...

Much Ado About Nothing

Is there bad energy in my house?
What about my car?
The answer is yes, if we believe it so,
if we take it that far.

Don't give credence to hypotheses,
all is well within your sphere.
Drop the meaning it's "this" or "that,"
presume your coast is clear.

♥ 💕 ♥

When you argue with reality, you're guaranteed to lose.

Why Fight?

Can we accept each happenstance
and trust it is what it is?
There is a course that life will take,
why counter what clearly exists?

There is no point, there is no use,
there is no value in fighting.
Should we rebel against the night sky
and tell the stars to stop shining?

What if what happens is for our good,
perhaps the Universe is benevolent?
Maybe there's nothing to add or subtract,
what if we've got all that's relevant?

♥ ❣ ♥

Life's too short to save for a rainy day.

Why Wait?

While waiting for that certain someone,
we may forget to live.
Next we know, life's passed us by,
and we've precious little to give.

Why save your life for a rainy day
when this is what you've got?
You possess within this moment
everything that you ought.

♥ ❣ ♥

À la carte

I used to complain until I realized,
it's like slapping God in the face.
It's like saying: I won't accept any gifts,
on me your time don't waste.

What if the predicament you're in right now
has been given to you for more—
more joy, more growth, more happiness, more peace
so why be upset, why be sore?

It's okay to feel bummed out for a while
but when you continue that mood,
you're robbing yourself of the opportunity to be
in joy and gratitude.

Why not thank these circumstances
for bringing you what you need.
It's a perfect and customized plan for you—
an à la carte menu, if you please.

♥ 💕 ♥

Pizza Delivery

Where is he?
That elusive mate.
"Hello? Pizza Delivery,
why must I wait?"

"I'll take one Beloved,
(hold the anchovies as I cut in line).
It is a simple order
when True Love is so inclined."

I opened up the menu,
a recipe appeared:
Give up, relax, look yourself in the eye—
Your Beloved is already here.

♥ ❧ ♥

sanity

then it dawned on me
(as i sat beneath the tree)
there's naught i need to know
and knowing naught
has set me free

♥ ❣ ♥

Groovy Baby

Do you find you judge yourself
for not having a quick enough wit?
Are you slow to end or start,
or is it you know when to quit?

The cadence of your wit is divine,
however fast you move.
Even when you're standing still,
your rhythm is in the groove.

♥ ❣ ♥

The Gift

This gift of life comes with a quota
of moments we can embrace.
To choose to worry or fret or suffer
would be a terrible waste.

♥ ♥ ♥

K.I.S.S.
(Keep It Simple Sweetie)

Why make it complicated—
do you really need something to fix?
Is that how you feel successful,
when you can gain something out of reach?

Are you creating unnecessary difficulties
so you can feel important and wise?
No need for you to flaunt those skills
when what's important is what's inside.

♥ ❥ ♥

Face Value

Things may not
be as they seem.
Do you know what's happening
behind the scenes?
What if everything's working
towards our dreams?

♥ 💕 ♥

EASY PEASY
(Shine On)

Easy Peasy, Lemon Squeezy,
What ya gonna do?
I've signed up for an easy life,
how about you?

When it's time for the sun to set
or hide behind a cloud,
its light is not snuffed out,
its brilliance is perfectly loud.

Life doesn't need to be that hard,
you have the tools in hand.
Even when you're feeling dim,
your light is eternally grand.

♥ ❥ ❤

Ego She Go

Sometimes I plainly don't want to think,
my Think Machine is tired.
I'll put my brain out to pasture,
consider myself retired.

Every once in a while, I may be obliged
to feed it a handful of words.
But goodness me, it thrives on noise
and will fight if it feels unheard.

♥ ❣ ♥

mindless

i can practice leaving behind
useless thoughts that constrict and bind
then a space will open wide
beyond the clutter of my mind

today i work without my ego
no efforts thoughts or concerning placebo
cruising in neutral control out of view
trading my disputes for a tranquil debut

♥ ♥ ♥

Mindless Too

When my mind goes astray
and I've lost my way
to places that were familiar,
it's disconcerting at the least
when you're used to a beast
of a brain that'd take you anywhere.

The synapses didn't fire,
I have a loose wire,
and I'm running on practically empty.
So I'll pull up a chair
(gaze into thin air)
and write poems that flow aplenty!

♥ 💕 ♥

A life lived in fear is no life at all...

Hobnob With Me

Who are you keeping company with?
I trust it's in your best interest.
When you're stuck, can't take that first step,
I'd venture you'd want something different.

Are you anticipating a meeting with Dread?
Why not convene with Optimism instead?
Living with Doom is no life at all,
Hope and Cheer will surely enthrall.

Yet, there's a level we could choose
where we anticipate nothing at all.
Here we don't worry what might be coming,
we're content with whatever befalls.

Who are you keeping company with,
are they adding to your peace?
I trust you know who to invite inside
for a life that's full of ease.

♥ ❥ ♥

Balancing Act

I have an affair with chocolate,
on occasion I'm tempted with wine,
but as my mum has always said:
with balance in life, you'll be fine.

The problem is (or is it a problem?)
my parts don't seem to cooperate.
When I try to strike a yoga pose
I end up quite immoderate!

Black or white, yep that's me,
I don't usually fall in between.
Finding a happy medium
is decidedly not my thing.

I'll take my extremes, especially in chocolate
or high-heeled dances in the rain.
I'll live each day like there's no tomorrow,
time and time again.

♥ ❣ ♥

Let things be, trust "what is." Feel your heart
open, no longer resist.

Unattached

Trust the way life is unfolding,
choose to accept it all.
Be open and curious, neutral and unbiased
even if the sky should fall.

It's not the end, and if it was,
is that so very bad?
When you're not attached to the outcome,
you'll find your heart is glad.

Everything you need for the life you want
is present within you now.
No need to seek or force or try,
just sit, relax, allow.

♥ ♥ ♥

The Way of Flow

On a blank slate, I long to write,
etching what I will.
Creating different aspects of scenes,
perspectives that fulfill.

Yet now is unique, I have decided,
upon this first step I know,
I need not design my way at all
as my way is The Way of Flow.

♥ ♥ ♥

Laughter's good medicine: "Take two teaspoons and call me in the morning."

Giggles & Guffaws

Don't be so serious, it's only a story,
sad, happy—we can choose.
When we know our story isn't real,
we'll surely be amused.

Grab a seat,
watch the show.
Laughter's good medicine
for when you're low.

From light giggles to guffaws,
expiratory actions are likely to cause
a cease in your suffering,
a much-needed pause.

Grab a seat,
watch the show.
A little laughter
will lighten your load.

♥ ❣ ♥

No Vex Flex

Trust life fully,
or you might as well be dead.
Why must you listen
to the voices in your head?

I don't know about you,
but my thoughts aren't always credible,
if I don't take them seriously,
life becomes more flexible!

♥ ❥ ♥

Silence is Golden

Many times when I reflect,
nothing useful arises.
Letting go of mindless chatter,
the silence quietly surprises.

Movement all around,
sounds that confound,
can you hear the quiet?

The hush that is your poise,
the silence behind the noise,
the relief beyond the riot.

♥ 💕 ♥

Can we trust everything is working towards our well-being?

The Tapestry of Life

Up, down, smile, frown,
it's all part of the design.
The Tapestry of Life that is,
which doesn't always align
with threads that are so fine and neat,
or an image that's complete.
But when it's time to turn the fabric,
you'll see a picture of flawless magic.

♥ 💘 ♥

Is it really true?

Loosey-Goosey

Just because you think it's true
doesn't make it so.
Seriousness can get you stuck,
loosen up to flow.

♥ 💕 ♥

When we strip away "our story" of who we think we are (parent, artist, success, failure...), what are we left with?

The Perfect Outfit

Are you truly this or that:
"inadequate," "inefficient," "incapable,"
or are they lies you've fallen for,
what if those labels aren't stable?

What if the truth is plainly this:
you're as perfect as when you were born,
flawless and whole, no matter what you've been told,
a completeness that's never outworn.

♥ ❥ ❤

Stand firm for the truth of who you are!

Make Your Mark

Why are you apologizing
for who and what you are?
You're doing the best that you can do,
why regret you've missed the mark?

Perhaps that mark
is not what you need.
Your higher self
knows how to proceed.

Every day and every way,
I'm getting better and better.
I'll not be sorry if to your standards
I simply didn't measure.

♥ ❦ ♥

Do Unto Others

What if we don't need forgiveness?
What if we're all enough?
Then no matter what we do,
there's no resentment—only Love.

♥ ❣ ❤

To Err is Human

Just because you say
it's outrageous
that she did that
with no remorse
to innocent ones without recourse—
forgive, for you are forgiven.

Just because you say
it's incredulous
that he did that
for so long and hidden,
God sees it in the blink of an eye—
forgive, for you are forgiven.

♥ ❣ ❤

Momentum

The remedy for inertia is action—
when you're stuck it's hard to begin.
Yet even a little movement
will gather momentum within.

Surrender the need to know what's ahead,
each moment will add to your day.
Before you know, you'll be out and about
designing your steps on the way.

♥ ❣ ♥

I practice being there for myself. I am my own best friend.

What If

What if I'm not important,
what if nobody cares?
Are my words insignificant,
is there no one there?

What if I drop definitions:
"important," "noteworthy," "esteemed,"
set about getting on with my life
with no need to be redeemed?

I'm choosing to be important
to myself who's always here.
I'll show up and be significant,
for me I'll lend an ear.

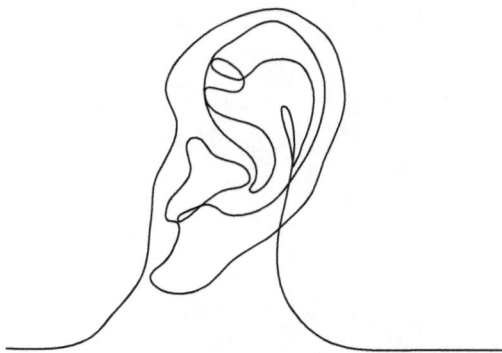

♥ 💋 ♥

More

Have you ever chased a bubble
only to watch it pop?
You saw it sail by,
first high in the sky,
and then to the ground did drop.

Our lives are like a bubble,
we're here and then we're not.
Do you chase for more
while your life ignore—
let's engage with what we've got.

♥ ♥ ♥

Non-Toxic

Since I stopped making meaning
of what others did or said,
my life is so much sweeter,
centered in my body, not my head.

Is it true I have an abuser,
or did I deem it so?
Is he truly a toxic person
or my thoughts that won't let go?

♥ 💕 ❤

Hurry Slowly

I love the phrase:
"Hurry Slowly as One."
When I listen, rather than act,
all that needs doing, gets done.

Hurry slowly—
let's ruminate on that,
take a moment to contemplate
what's needed for this task?

With presence and awareness,
there's no need for effort or scurry.
When we choose to take some space,
we'll find no room for worry.

Darling, let's not ruin our health
and forget what we must do:
focus our valuable attention
on enjoying this current view.

♥ ♥♥ ♥

Rise Above

Take everything lightly
the sun will likely
rise again.

Make the most of every day,
and if you don't,
then that's ok.

♥ ꒰ ♥

Self-Absorbed or Self-Love

It's rather addictive sitting here,
in my room unrestricted with no one near.

I'm plugging in to hoards of plenty,
on social media that's filling me empty.

It's somewhat quiet here you see,
until a "like" ends my reverie.
And thus confirms It's All About Me!

♥ ❣ ♥

Directions

How do we arrive at a happy life?
Be content with where you are.
But what should we do to get to that place?
Nothing! It's here, not far.

♥ ❣ ❤

Inner peace is an inside job.

MY COMPANIONS
(Sit Inside Your Being)

What does this mean:
"Sit inside your Being."
Rather, what is the feeling
this statement is revealing?

It conjures up for me
an image of a chair
in a wide-open space
filled with clear, fresh air.

My Being is empty
except for the chair,
upon which I sit
and there's nothing else there.

You might feel this is
a sad and lonely place,
yet in this central void,
Inner Peace exists with Grace.

♥ ♥ ♥

We don't know what's going on in the heart of another. Can we respond with acceptance?

COUNTERPOISE
(Tea and Sympathy)

He blocks my way,
can't let me succeed.
His need for control
won't let him concede.

A cup of compassion
is in my heart for you
when you get your fix
the way you do.

I choose to go
on my Merry Way
as love is the response
I give today.

♥ 💕 ♥

Many Paths — Same Sky

Do you have a destination in mind?
There are many ways to consider.
Is it the hard beaten path you find
or the easy flowing river?

Do you walk or fly with the stars,
are there signs along the road?
Do you let Life choose the way
and rest in that perfect abode?

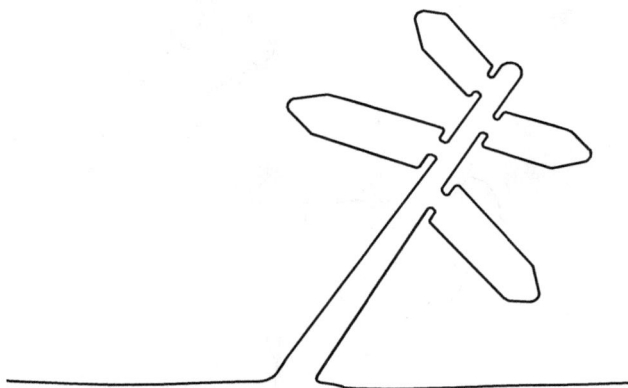

♥ 💕 ♥

The Gentle Gardener

My lush landscape trampled with your words,
harshness uprooted the tender saplings.
They reached for the sun, amidst your clouds.

I cultivate my garden with gentle hands,
roses and weeds greet with kindred smiles.
In this land of mixed blooms, kindness will prevail.

♥ ❧ ♥

Topsy-Turvy

When things are wonky
and the world's topsy-turvy,
perk up, it ain't gonna last.
Today's funk is tomorrow's lunch,
no need to be aghast.

Let's watch with curiosity
when the way we choose feels dark.
Curiosity is our ally,
creating adventures to embark.

♥ ♥ ♥

Did they abandon you, or did you abandon yourself?

Mainstay

I choose me in my messy sprawl,
I choose me when I'm contracted and small.
I'm my best friend, my comfort and guide,
my own secure anchor when others collide.

♥ ❥ ♥

The Voices in My Head

All-at-once I discovered:
Where I go there I am.
I'm a one-stop-comedy-shop;
a one-woman sham.

I'm entertainment on wheels,
the vehicle is me,
the driver's out to lunch;
vacant passengers agree.

No need to step outside,
a barrel of laughs I find
inside the nooks and crannies
of my thoroughly amusing mind.

♥ ♥ ♥

Patience

What's the end? Tell me.
What do I need?

Quiet now, wait and see—
tall plants begin as seed.

♥ ❤ ♥

OF LOVE AND WAR
(Coming Home)

A weary traveler of threescore and more
traversed countless roads of Love and War
in order to find a home that many
would discover once in a lifetime, if any.

Upon arriving to where he began,
he happened on a Wise Old Man:
"You need not travel far and wide
for home is the heart where you reside."

♥ ❣ ♥

"Right" or "Wrong" is a matter of perception.
Choose to grab life fully and see what befalls!

THE "RIGHT" PATH
(The Way)

There's no use fighting
The Way that is meant.
Embrace and allow
the perfection that is sent.

Whether the path feels easy
is entirely up to you,
it's all about perception,
how you describe your view.

I've chosen my path,
The Way feels light,
grateful for each step
with no end in sight.

♥ ♥ ♥

Love and hate, peace and terror—simply different sides of the same coin.

yin and yang

within failure is success
within sorrow there's happiness

within fear is courage and heart
the sun rises in contrast to dark

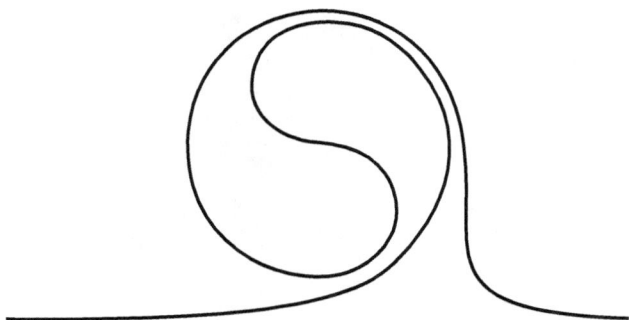

♥ ❥ ❤

Fails With Flying Colors

Do we ever truly fail?
I'd say it's a matter of perception.
"Failures," "triumphs,"
merely words...
Failure is success in action.

♥ 💕 ❤

KINDLING
(Earth Angel)

The Universe tickles me with her mirth
when once I declared: "I have everything of worth,
I need nothing and want no other,
within my Being is the Perfect Lover!"

Then an Earth Angel came up my path
and presented himself (much to my wrath).
Now I writhe with unquenchable desire,
he scratched the itch of this bottomless mire.

These days I furrow my brow almost hourly
with an explicit longing that borders on cowardly.
I fear I'll never have this dance,
the pleasures of your perfect romance.

So I succumb to the quiet and sweet,
to the nothingness lying beneath my feet.
The no one, the person, the object of my desire,
as I look again to rekindle my fire.

♥ ❣ ♥

In hindsight I realize I'm already complete.

Twenty-twenty

Do you see it? Pay attention—
it's nearer than you think.
Feel now, hush now,
there is no missing link.

The vision, the revelation,
this enlightenment that is you
is already completely yours—
there's nothing you need to do.

♥ 💕 ♥

True rest is when we stop seeking.

Calm Rapids

The Eternal You
has nothing to seek.
The steady, undisturbed you
is always at peace.

Going against the grain
adds nothing but grief.
Flowing with Life's river
is such a relief!

♥ ❣ ♥

Laissez-Faire

To force is not of Flow,
be loose like undone string.
Hands off, rest now,
you have everything you need.

Wherever life does take me,
I promise I'll be there.
The door is open to joy and peace,
and presence is what I wear.

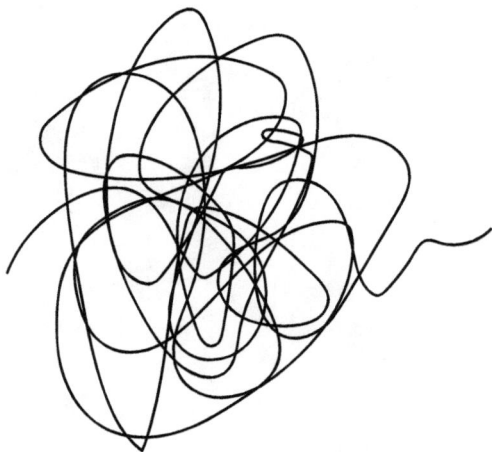

♥ ❣ ❤

I can choose to speak kindly to myself.

Get Lost!

When the voices in my head
start to speak unkindly,
I tell them go and take a hike,
your words are quite untimely.

♥ 💕 ♥

Ignorance is bliss.

The City of Wonder

This City of Wonder I live in
is quite the trip of glee.
A magical ride on the road Unknown
to the place of No Guarantee.

♥ ❧ ❤

Take the day off!

Let Go

Will the gardens grow,
will the rivers flow,
will the earth keep turning
if I let go?

Imagine feeling safe
at home within your skin
that nothing and no one can shake
the peace that dwells within.

♥ ♥ ♥

let go even more

a man once taught me
to give him all my weight
stop holding myself up
let go don't hesitate

i will hold you
ease up
soften
just be
notice any tension
release into me

♥ 💕 ♥

What you consider your weakness could indeed be your strength.

Celebrate You

Celebrate each "weakness,"
you can store them up at length,
to be given away to others
who consider them as strengths.

♥ ❣ ❤

Carpe Diem

By the time you finish reading this line,
it's already in the past.
We have but a few moments in life,
savor them; they don't last.

The days fly by like pages of a book
upon which the wind has caught.
I catch a glimpse of a Saturday in May
and realize my worries were for naught.

♥ 💕 ♥

Let it be...

Sans Souci

If I could live amongst the trees
to exist as home for birds and bees...
With no fight to reach the top
they let things be, to thrive or not.

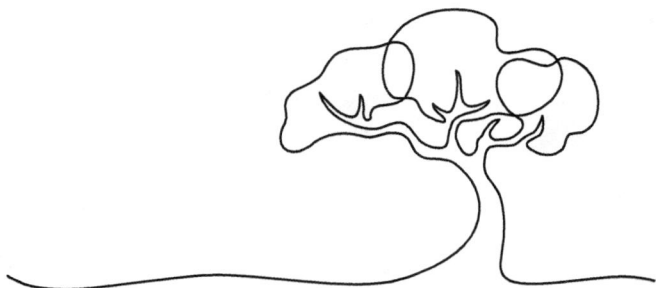

Discontent is not a thing
be they green, brown, thick or lean.
If I could live amongst the trees,
perhaps I'd rest and leave things be.
Disenchantment would leave my side
in this world of green where I reside.

If I could live amongst the trees
to exist as home for birds and bees...
With no fight to reach the top
they let things be, to thrive or not.

♥ ♥♥ ♥

wheat and chaff

today i let go
more than before
and notice what remains
the essence of me
continues to be
free of that which constrains

♥ 💕 ♥

You love me because you are Love. I love you because I am Love.

It Is Enough

When you say, "It's not enough,
I'm not loved like this or that."
Please remember each of us
loves as much as we can love,
and that is it, and that is enough.

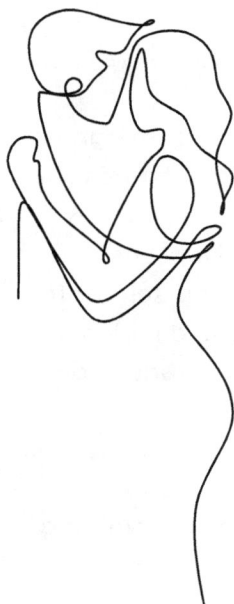

♥ 💕 ♥

It doesn't make sense, you say?—How wonderful!

NONSENSE
(The Place to Be)

When nothing makes sense,
choose to let things go.
Do your best to trust
the Greater Power that knows.

This path makes no sense
yet stick around and see,
that Nowhere as a destination
is surely The Place to Be.

A road named Nonsense
can guide you to rest
to experience the nothingness
that will bring you the best.

On The Way of Nonsense
where you find yourself for free,
close your eyes and look again—
everything is as meant to be.

When the weary day is starting,
unsure of what's ahead,
you'll surely find that Nothing
will tuck you back in bed!

♥ ❣ ♥

Moonlight Kisses

Tonight you walked down those stairs
your naked body
and the cool night air,
to the Universe's kisses.

You felt them like dew upon your skin
moistening and cherishing the nourishment within.
Kisses that spoke words of comfort,
letting you know we are triumphant.

We see your smile,
it comes from the heart,
you light up the sky
with stars and night art.

We see you and thank you
for simply being you.
You're pure, you're connected,
you know what's true.

Relax, let us hold you,
let us hold you up.
Let go, fall into our arms,
we'll never shut you up.

We'll never hurt you,
you can trust that too.
Because we love,
the way you do.

You can count on us,
your God who hears,
we're the Universe and gentle forces—
release your fears.

We will always uphold you,
we will always keep you safe.
We're soft, we're kind,
you're The One we celebrate.

When you felt the night air
on your naked body tonight
that was us kissing you,
whispering everything's alright.

So, soften your heart,
it got a little tight there;
it makes sense
when you're stripped bare.

Please open again,
you know you can.
Be open and vulnerable,
we're holding your hand.

We're just like you,
loving completely and true.
We know you don't understand
why they hurt you as they do.

You see they hurt,
they can't let go,
what they do is lash out;
we're sorry it was so.

We're sorry he did that,
and we forgive him too,
just like you forgive him,
because we are you.

We're just like you,
you can count on that.
We delight in you—
on that hang your hat.

♥ ♥ ♥

Loving What Is

Out of the mud I breathe,
out of nothing I become...
Acceptance With Joy.

♥ ❣ ❤

*There's nowhere to go, there's nothing to know,
you're where you need to be.*

"Stand At Ease"

Circumstances are
as they need to be,
because they are—
because they're decreed.

Contentment is
being happy with this.
Celebrate it all—
there's nothing to resist.

♥ ❣ ❤

The Future of Now

Future, a figment of imaginations...
Ruminating, my mind twisted into contortions.
Then I remember The Gift of Now,
and in that moment, I gracefully bow.

No plans, no goals—
Be Here Now.
No dreams or ambitions,
simply Live and Allow.

♥ ♥ ♥

We're never too old to play.

Dilly-Dally

Dabble, Dawdle, Dilly-Dally—
lather, rinse, repeat.
Happiness will be your tune
when logic's obsolete.

No more judging harshly,
I'll move at my own pace.
Loving my silly stories
and nonsensical debate.

With multiple stops along the way,
I'll take this time to pause...
and follow Imagination,
leaving Sensible and Practical lost.

I've no ambition to reach the top,
exploring Come What May.
Allowing my whims to carry me
where Reasoning's gone to play.

♥ ❥ ♥

Nichey Glitchy

Are you truly being authentic
or do you bend to another?
Might you start to find the strength
to face the truth you uncover?

Hear and feel the perfect pitch
that only you can know.
Finely tuned for your sweet niche,
fits with room to grow.

To the harmony of your soul be true,
to that song you know is you—
the melody that vibrates in kind...
sound waves resonate and align.

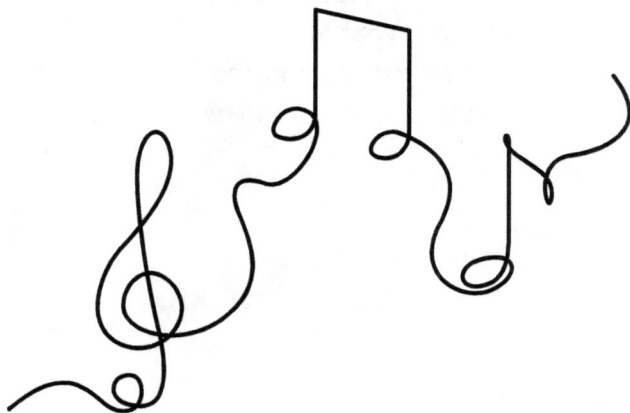

♥ ˙♥ ♥

No one can hurt me—that's my job!

Sticks and Stones

Listening to my body,
not the stories in my head,
I stopped making meaning
of what others did or said.

My days are so much easier
when my mind is peace and quiet,
I no longer take offense
to another's inner riot.

♥ 💕 ♥

a moment in time

you see a barren mess
barely a green shoot showing
have you seen the master plan
everything you need is growing

relax don't fret your heart
pull up your easy chair
life is working behind the scenes
with fulfillment beyond compare

enjoy the sights along the way
there's nothing that needs to be found
tomorrow will come another day
be present to what abounds

♥ ❥ ♥

Goldilocks

Too small, too large,
too soft, too hard—
it takes me a while to feel
settled and safe
in a new place;
I see more than eyes can reveal.

I sense what's above,
below and around,
unseen to all but me.
I'm highly sensitive
with gifted discernment—
precisely as I need be.

♥ ❥ ♥

All that needs doing gets done...

BIT BY BIT
(One Bite at a Time)

I'm desperate, needing assurance,
at home with too many cares.
Overwhelmed, so much to do,
alone with unanswered prayers.

Feeling stuck, where to begin?
I'm told—this too shall pass.
All will fall into place,
the misery we feel won't last.

How do we eat an elephant?
We take one bite at a time!
Trusting the Universe has our back,
as we shift our paradigm.

♥ 💕 ♥

Section 3

The Promise

"I feel heard, seen, and understood by me."
—Shira Bliss

How do you feel treasured and loved?—Do it first for yourself.

Show up for yourself, prove to yourself over and over that you can count on yourself. This kindness to you takes practice, and practice makes perfect. You don't have to go far to get this valuable service, because wherever you go, there you are!

When we practice being present for ourselves and allowing things to be as they are, we can then fully celebrate ourselves and this wonderful life we've been gifted with.

You are The One.

LOVE SONG
(To The Beloved Within)

I see you.
Your tears have not gone unnoticed.
They feel like dew
cleansing me,
dripping over my body.

Come to me now.
Don't be afraid.
Open your flower,
breathe into your heart,
come within.

My heart opens and I recognize
the depth, the breadth, the length of you.
I love how you love,
I desire to love you,
I will love you.

Thank you for opening.
Your beauty is seen.
Dive deeply, I'm here.
Dive deeply my sweet love.
I will not go away.

♥ ♥ ♥

Sailing

When you catch wind
of who you are,
your sails will supremely soar.
There's nothing to prove,
you are enough,
simply because you were born.

As you sail the seas
of peace and ease,
your ship has now come in.
The wholeness that's you
has come into view,
your life will now begin.

♥ ❣ ♥

*When I stop looking outside for fulfillment,
I find the abundance within.*

NO PLACE LIKE HOME
(Lush and Lively)

If I were not me,
I would wish to be
this one that lives herein.

The grass is green
on my side of the fence,
lush and lively within!

♥ ❥ ❤

Damn Good

As I rummage about within the depths of me,
I excavate and discover those aspects of glee
that touch and possess each part of me...

Bubbling slowly and then to a frenzy,
encompassing my being like no other entity,
stimulating, populating, nourishing and satisfying
these subjects and volumes of libraries inside.

When I walk about (or sit or stand),
the moments I have are incredibly grand.
I love this life, this one with me;
within captivity, I'm delightfully free.

In me, right now, is everything I need
to last me a lifetime, to satisfy my greed,
to suckle every drop of juice that I meet
and tap into the richness sitting at my feet.

This sweet completeness, I breathe it in,
magnify it, feel it in my tummy and in my chin,
here now, I'm captivated
by the bliss that I'm in.

As I rummage about within the depths of me,
I excavate and discover those aspects of glee
that touch and possess each part of me.

Feels so damn good!

♥ ❣ ♥

*"One derogatory word from you and I'm crushed.
One statement of praise and I'm elated."*

Damage and Reparation

*Joy is found in tiny crevices,
the dust of which is swept away
by one phrase from a lover's mouth.*

Just because they say it,
doesn't mean it's true.
Your worth doesn't change
when others judge you.

Remember the day you were told
that your smile lit up the room—
it still does.

♥ 💕 ♥

No Sweeter Sound

When you speak,
nations shudder with relief,
and they sigh in contented bliss
if graced with one single kiss
from you.

The lilt of your voice
no sweeter sound has ever been heard.
A song above the birds of all the flocks.
Even gods listen with bended ears
as time stops.

♥ ♥ ♥

The Whole Gamut

With you, I learned how it feels to be satisfied
and for that I was thankful.
With me, I learned how it feels to be satisfied—
deeper, broader, wider
and for that I am thankful.

With open eyes, I now can see
the colors of every rainbow.
I feel the tones of all the music,
the contrasts of light and shadow.

I am a cherry tree
basking beneath my blossoms.
The sweet scent of all that's divine,
I'm sunshine and tulips and poppies.

♥ 💕 ♥

Despite perceived loss or gain, the inner bliss within remains.

Who Am I?

I'm not this current story
even though it's told so well.
I'm not labels and perceptions
my mind makes up to tell.

I am what cannot be taken away,
I am true love and peace.
I am pure light and dark,
I am what cannot cease.

♥ ❥ ♥

The truest love song you'll ever sing is the one you sing to yourself.

This Love Within

Your voice
in my breath
soothes my pain.
The cadence of your song
comforts my longing
and fills
my empty places.

All my dreams
feature you.
I see you
and I touch your face.
I fall
into
your
embrace.

You are mine,
I am yours
Nothing to explain—
you remain.

I believe you,
I trust you,
I will not abandon you.
I come to you,
there is none else.
This Love Within.

♥ ♥♥ ♥

If it's meant to be, it will be. If it's meant for us, it is ours.

Flow

Today I'm water,
I gracefully flow,
trusting the process
with no need to know.

Water takes the shape it goes,
it doesn't question how to flow,
nor does it strive to change the climate,
instead it allows a natural alignment.

♥ ꕥ ♥

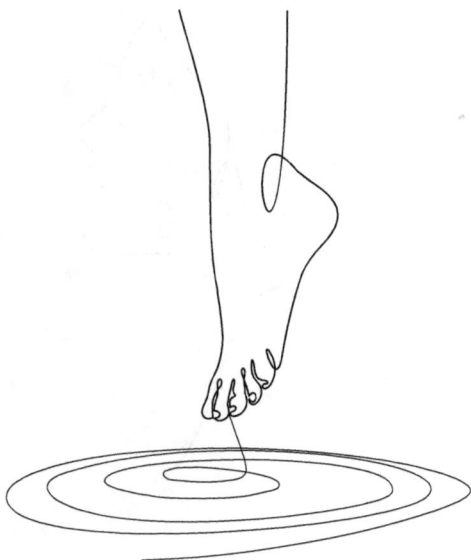

Pure Gold

Leisurely mornings, leisurely days,
I sure do love my leisurely ways.
It's such a gift to have this freedom
after years of striving, being so driven.

Each moment was filled
with children and bills,
now the space inside
has me feeling fulfilled.

This is a gift not taken for granted,
it appears my ship has finally landed.
My wish for you is to remember gladness,
just look inside, beneath the sadness.

Amongst the fierce noise and eager bustle,
there's a gentle place, away from the hustle.
The ease and grace that you can find
within yourself is a pure gold mine.

♥ ♥ ♥

Soliloquy

I like watching
my pen stroke the page,
flowing like silk,
my soliloquy assuaged.

I like writing,
exposing thoughts contained,
sitting and contemplating,
nonsense and reality exchanged.

♥ ♥ ♥

STEP INSIDE
(A Thousand Kisses)

Let me kiss you with kisses so sweet,
the dew on all the flowers can't compete.
Let me cover your skin with my true embrace
and delight in each aspect of your shape.

Let me kiss you with kisses so tender,
La Petite Mort upon you render.
We'll visit other spheres to greet
the soft petals and riches at our feet.

I've died a thousand deaths you know
to arise with the strength that you bestow,
nourished by your graceful fluids
that moisten, revive, and render me lucid.

I've died a thousand deaths and each time I awake,
it's to your voice I tremble and shake
with the most glorious and profound images of late—
great men and mountains and magnificent states.

Let me kiss you with a thousand kisses,
let me nourish you with the desire of my wishes.
May I kiss you, as words subside,
would you allow me to step inside?

♥ ꒰ ♥

Kinship

Through your eyes
I watch us shine.
Your heart and mine
we intertwine.

I am you, you are me,
together we meet in unity.
Blossoms flourish where we step
in life's garden as we connect.

♥ ❣ ❤

There is only one. There is no other.

Unity

I have my place
in love I align.
Your spirit is yours,
my experience is mine.

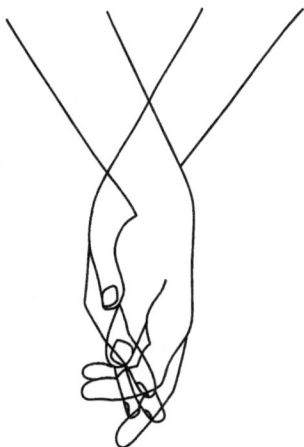

I have my place—
what does that mean?
It means I know where I end
and where you convene.

I'm in my body (this here and now)
first gathering my parts
that have fragmented, and allow
the dark and the light, the day and the night
to put aside their weary fight.

I have my place
in love I align.
Your spirit is yours,
my experience is mine.

♥ 💕 ♥

Cold was a frequent visitor, until I made room for warmth.

The Warmth of You

Nestled between you and me
is the piece that fills my spaces,
stay with me, my skin is cold,
I need your warm embraces.

Nestled between me and you
are oceans quiet and furious,
ever changing, ever the same,
your waves of love victorious.

Nestled between us is sweetness,
as sweet as a child is known,
a sweetness that flirts to linger
and leaves me less alone.

Nestled between you and me is nothing
and everything and all good things...
a contented sigh as you nuzzle my neck,
sinking deeply into dreams.

Of teddy bears and kindness,
the sheltering from the storm,
I'll move a thousand mountains
to climb to your sacred warmth.

♥ ❧ ♥

I Ride on Your Words

I ride on your words—
those tasty morsels of you,
as they travel from your throat
and out your mouth as dew.

Resting a while, I luxuriate
on your luscious, succulent lips,
'til those delicious utterances
moisten my pores like mist.

Nourishing me, kissing my mouth,
they move into my heart,
claiming every inch of my being,
delighting in doing their part.

Your laugh, I taste it:
The Nectar of the Gods.
You're gentle Mother Earth,
Father Sky, the promise of above.

You're the start and the finish,
the sun that set and rose...
the boy who moves me to my core
with playfulness between his toes.

♥ ❣ ♥

First Kiss

Nothing is better
than that first kiss.
Or, could it be...
the more kisses
the deeper the bliss.

♥ ❣ ♥

speechless

he rendered me speechless
with his kiss
a feat that's not easy
to command this bliss

upon the touching
of his lips to mine
my myriads of words
are now reclined

♥ ♥ ♥

Engaging my senses, one-by-one...

The Sense of Bliss

A plate of food before me—
I use my eyes to explore;
focus on the various hues,
senses imploring for more.

I practice separating the smells—
savory, sweet, and salt;
I touch the food as if my lover,
his words I crave to exalt.

Next I taste,
my delight begins to grow,
first as a tickle,
then a delicious glow.

Increasing like a blush
up my body to my cheeks,
tingling in each of my fingertips
and places beyond my reach.

Then I cry a happy moan
over the food that I prepare,
in my sunshiny kitchen
with no one and me to share.

Together we elope
to the land of milk and tears,
of joy and latent laughter,
of love and long-lost years.

♥ ❦ ♥

What's my purpose?
To love and be loved.

Spot-On!

Today I design my steps with no purpose—
no plans, no goals, no game.
Extending love simply to love,
spot-on without an aim.

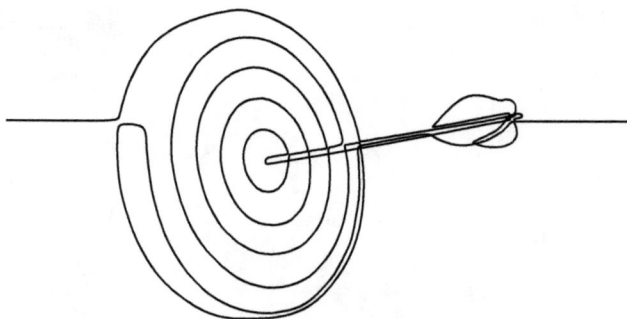

♥ 💕 ♥

Even when alone, I am connected.

The Forest of Knowing

I am a tree,
a green succession of thickness,
intrinsically connected,
majestic, filled with richness.

Nothing can thwart me,
I'm nourished and nourishing,
continually growing
in strength, I'm flourishing.

Animals live in my branches,
fruit is abundant from my tree,
in this forest of fortitude
no longer alone with me.

♥ 💕 ♥

Enchanté

When the outer disappears,
the inner becomes
your deepest enchantment.

The enchantment of you,
a marriage of light and dark,
a secret gallery of holy art.

♥ 💕 ♥

embracing my age

my unadorned self
embraces the grace
and cherishes the gray
that crowns my face

proud of the wisdom
woven into my uniqueness
relishing in the splendor
of my simple completeness

♥ 💕 ♥

When you're happy with who you are, it won't matter who isn't.

Organic

There's nothing to do,
no need to add more.
Unapologetically me,
right down to my core.

Releasing the need to shine,
I take this moment to drop
the desire to "accomplish" anything,
I'll rest now, yes I'll stop.

Adding another notch
to feed this ego of mine,
yet there's no need of anything
for the organic me to shine.

*You're the same innate being
since arriving here on earth,
if placed before a judge,
could he prove you're not of worth?*

"Your Honor, based on the evidence
that this person is alive,
we determine she is good enough,
good enough to thrive."

I was born who I am, I will die who I am,
nothing and no one will change that.
My existence, my spirit, is beyond perceptions,
nothing and no one will rearrange that.

♥ ❥ ♥

Innie Outie

The Inner Voice
inspires me with silence,
takes my hand,
comforts and enlivens.

Outside voices
become the noise,
my inner self
is my balance and poise.

♥ ❥ ❤

A to B

there's nowhere to go
there's nothing to know
i'm where i need to be

this place where i am
is precisely the plan
to get me from A to B

♥ ❣ ♥

There's always something to be thankful for.

full days

birdsong and croaking frogs
the smell of a crisp ocean breeze
carries me on days that are full
bursting at the seams

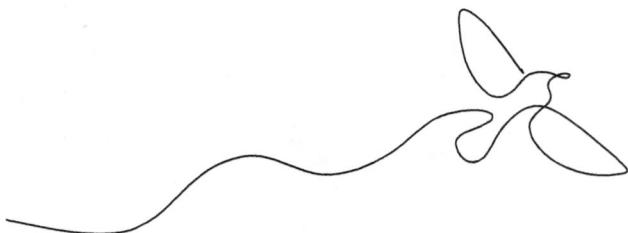

♥ ❣ ❤

Let go of becoming anything. Just Be LOVE.

I Am Love

While trying to become something,
I've let go of everything
as I realize I am nothing—
just Love.

♥ ❣ ❤

Ode to my French Toast...

EASY
(Breakfast in Bed)

Waking up is easy
when I'm waking up to you.
Your smell, the tantalization
as you dance on my taste buds.
I want to inhale you, devour you...
Yet I know if I do,
then it'll be over—
this feast of sensuality
that plays a symphony on my lips
and enlivens the synapses of my being.

So I pace myself,
no longer careening through life
grabbing at every experience.
I realize now there is nothing to add
as I am the addition,
the addition of One:
The sum of All.
And, I am satisfied.
Yes, I am satisfied.

♥ ❣ ❤

Take life "as is," even when uncomfortable...

WINDS OF CHANGE
(Reassurance on a Blustery Day)

The winds of change are here,
they've always been a constant.
One moment it's glassy waters,
the next, a storm is rampant.

Why not count those "ups" and "downs"
and trust them all as "up"?
When we believe it's all meant to be
we'll have our cup filled up!

♥ ❣ ❤

Let Them Be

In my old age
I've grown to be
confident to know
what works for me.

Different strokes for different folks,
on that we'd surely agree.
I'll not judge you nor expect you to conform—
remain as you need be.

♥ ❥ ❤

Hunky-Dory

The leaves glisten on the trees:
"We're brand-new," they whisper.
Birds rise from slumber and sing:
"The concrete and clouds are crisper."

I've heard about a silver lining,
but what if it's pink or gray?
Perhaps it's a rainbow of colors
at certain times of the day.

I'll take what I can,
I've certainly had many
dreams that came true
and notions aplenty.

It's a peaceful place inside my head;
my expectations are no longer leading.
As long as the leaves, the birds and the bees
keep talking, I'll keep agreeing.

♥ ❣ ❤

A Pleasant Pause

I feel like I've had
a glorious day,
noted my "To Do" list
with frolic and play.

Items that pulled my attention
are not important it seems.
I'll drop the desire to ponder
on how to fulfill my schemes.

In the end my dreams
were filling up my head,
there's much more space
when I send them off to bed!

♥ 💕 ♥

Weather Report: Calm with Showers of Bliss

There's nothing to report,
for that my body sings.
My skin and bones are quiet,
blissful calm within remains.

♥ ❣ ♥

Lazy is the place to be...

Quiet and Space

I'm stuck to the couch with lazy glue,
it's a perfectly viable thing to do.
Or not do, as this is the case
when I gift myself this well-deserved space.

♥ 💕 ♥

Perfectly Imperfect

"How is your day?"
Nothing spectacular
and perfectly imperfect
in its own special way.

"How are you?"
Nothing spectacular
and perfectly imperfect
enjoying my view.

♥ ❥ ♥

peachy

appreciation is like a peach
nourishing, satisfying and pleasantly sweet
whether we give or choose to receive
appreciation branches out to please

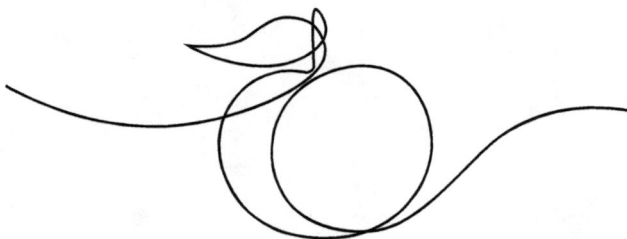

♥ ❣ ❤

Happy To Be

I'm getting younger
by the day,
at least that's what
I like to say!

When I see my reflection,
I click on a filter,
so I can pretend
to look a lot better.

Now that I'm old,
I don't give a damn,
I'm at peace
with who I am.

♥ 💕 ♥

Love Makes the World Go 'Round

Often I'm amazed,
(when into your eyes I gaze)
after ten plus years,
I'm comforted by your ways.

Our lives are better, because we're together;
we've grown in leaps and bounds.
With countless pleasures, adventures and treasures,
our love makes the world go 'round.

♥ 💕 ♥

Love Affairs

I fall in love most every day,
today it's with biscotti.
Many items catch my eye,
yesterday was coffee.

I've chosen to make my life a romance
with one thing or another.
I find sweet love in inanimate objects
and joy in every corner.

❤ ❥ ❤

Be True to You

Don't hide your True Self—
you're exactly what you need.
Don't change to appease another,
who needs you to be you indeed.

♥ 💕 ♥

You are Ideal

What if you are loved,
no matter what is said?
Loved, even to the contrary
of the voices in your head.

Accepting the perfection of who you are
is your shiny see-through-shield.
This keeps you safe from words or deeds
that imply you're less-than-ideal.

♥ ❣ ♥

Dedicated to the perfect love within.

My Perfect Love

You shine with a brilliance
that's connected
to all that's brilliant.
I'm exquisitely enchanted
by the way you move.

You are grace embodied.
Your joy fills my soul
with completeness.
You're the sun, the moon and stars,
you're everything, because you are.

Touched to my core,
I experience
all deliciousness within.
Because of you
delight spills forth from my Being.

I hear the gentle strumming within;
I feel your mesmerizing touch.
Soothing me, filling me,
down my back, in my heart,
coursing through every part.

Stimulating. Satisfying.
Beyond contentment, otherworldly.
I eat this up, my nourishment,
I carry this within my heart.
And you come to me.

♥ ❣ ♥

How we see each other is a choice...

Fresh Eyes

Each moment I see you anew,
though we're together every day.
Open mind, blank slate—
I prefer it be that way.

I clear the thoughts that went before
and open up the sliding door
to my inner sanctuary
where I don't keep score.

♥ 💕 ❤

Timeless

Live life loosely
"this too shall pass."
Whether we deem moments "good" or "bad,"
time is short; it won't last.

It's such a relief to know:
all is temporary.
When faced with what to be in life,
only love is necessary.

♥ ♥ ♥

YOU are the best thing that has ever happened to you!

CHOOSE YOU!
(The Perfect Date)

Do you love you most of all,
or do you prefer another?
What would it take to make the shift
to love you like no other?

You can be, your most desired,
this gift to yourself you can give.
Take the cue of loving you—
methinks it's the way to live!

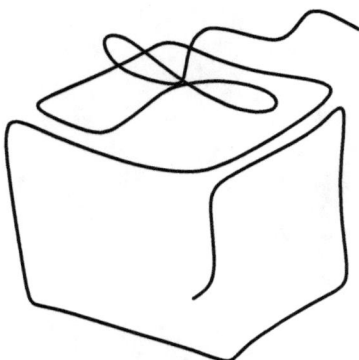

♥ ❣ ♥

cozy and poetry

often times
I have nothing to say
instead I get cozy
put off and delay
my worklist and I
laze about and play
with rhymes and silliness
blowing cobwebs away

♥ ❣ ♥

Assembled

I feel you reaching out,
gathering up my pieces.
Fragments brought from faraway places,
'til I merge cohesive.

You feel me watching you,
contentment on my face.
Mending seams, sharing life,
undone, stitched up, in place.

♥ ♥ ♥

Near & Far

I've loved you from afar
with arms that cradle your heart.
I've loved you from my sleep
awakened so I can reach
your moonlight visage
this rapture of mine—
the euphoria I long to keep.

♥ ❣ ❤

Arrived

Where is it that you want to be?
Perhaps you're there already.
Take a look, and you will see
the view is calm and steady.

In case you missed it, take the scenic route
for a life that's full and free.
This place isn't far, you won't need a car,
you're where you need to be.

♥ ❥ ♥

Now, I talk to myself the way I would to the child I love.

Arms Open Wide

Do you hear the music?
Listen even more and you will.
Feel
Be
Open
It's closer than you think.
Let the melody
rock you gently
in my arms of love.

♥ ♥ ♥

We Are Home

Smile upon us, sleepy gnome,
we are weary, bring us home.
Smile upon us, sleepy gnome,
help us realize we are home.

A sleepy gnome has found his place
upon a rock where none can face
the mischievous deeds that had to be done,
within this tale that must be spun.

Today and tomorrow, there's only one
to accomplish the needs of those that shun
the laying of his head upon his chin
where gods of men reside within.

A lowly snail has come to visit,
and finds the host reclined a minute.
He sleeps, perchance may not awaken,
the bedded heart fully broken and shaken,
to the ends of earth from start to finish
where all that's left is a single grimace.

Tomorrow again, he will begin
to smile those smiles he stored within
and grant you all your heart desires—
just stay awhile before he tires.

Smile upon us, sleepy gnome,
we are weary, bring us home.
Smile upon us, sleepy gnome,
help us realize we are home.

♥ ❤' ♥

Unparalleled

An incomparable instrument
is who and what you are.
You're not like any other,
making melodies near and far.

You are here to play the music
that can only flow through you.
You're a vessel tuned to perfection,
an exquisite, unparalleled debut.

♥ ❣ ♥

warm and golden

dear love
you are more than this
the threads of your skin and bones
are the gold fibers
that command this world
of mine
of yours

♥ ❥ ♥

If you were to describe yourself from Truth/God's perspective, what would you say?

True Love

True Love lets go of expectations.
True Love doesn't hold on to perceptions.
True Love celebrates the blossoming of another
even if she looks like a garden of weeds...
That garden of weeds can nourish a neighborhood.

♥ ❥ ♥

I've Got You

I will protect you
Don't run away
Stay a while
Feel me
Feeling you
Loving you
Caressing you
Let go
There is no need
Right now
Relax
I've got you.

♥ ♥ ♥

Relish please; hold the mayo.

Cherished

Once was lost,
didn't know where to look
to find those riches within.
Then I realized I'm right here,
relish in the treasure therein.

♥ 💕 ♥

SIT WITH ME
(Lullaby of Friday)

Would you care to stop
for a moment and drop
all activity and sit a while?
Let go of your fuss,
dispense with the rush,
I'll sing you songs with style.

It's not a trap,
I won't kidnap,
it'll be painless, I promise.
I'll feed you tea,
sweet as need be
and order your tomorrows.

♥ ♥♥ ♥

We are separate, yet connected.

Oneness

When one weeps,
the other tastes salt.
When "we" dissolve,
there is no fault.

There's only one,
there is no other,
no beginning or end,
only love to discover.

Searching for love until I realized,
love was here all the time.
Wherever I go, there I am—
I am love, love is mine.

♥ ❥ ❤

My borders have dissolved in the full color world of my reflection.

Full Color

In the mirror of the night,
I saw myself in black and white.
Upon the dawn, my heart did see
a splendid portrait that looked like me.

My outline is grand, it fills all space,
I've become an expanse of love and grace.
I do not know where I may end,
I only know myself as friend.

♥ ❥ ❤

Selfishly Giving

Do you have trouble receiving?
Consider this a fact:
whenever you accept,
you're actually giving back.

When I give to you,
it gives me great pleasure,
a favor you're doing
when you receive without measure.

I don't need a return,
just the chance to be
a giver to you
so I can receive.

♥ ❥ ♥

Why am I here?
To enjoy and be enjoyed.

Kismet

I make love
to what is.
Everything that happens
becomes my greatest gift.

I make love with life,
and life makes love with me.
I trust the process—
it's all meant to be.

♥ 💕 ♥

Self-Talk

Your inner voice is your best friend,
the source of unlimited wisdom.
Listen to that voice of peace,
show her that she's welcome.

♥ ❣ ❤

Nowhere Land

In doing nothing,
all gets done.
Everything works out
in the long run.

Nowhere Land—
it's the place to be.
You can get there by traveling
this world with me.

In this land you can choose
the path of ease.
It may not make sense,
there are no guarantees.

In doing nothing,
all gets done.
Everything works out
in the long run.

♥ ♥ ♥

I am my Beloved and my Beloved is mine.

Heart's Song

My dearest friend, my sweetest love,
I feel your touch profoundly.
Passing through dimensions with no name,
sleep has awakened me soundly.

The angels told me they hear my song,
I need not say a word.
I am the melody, I am the silence,
I am the music unheard.

♥ 💕 ♥

Hush now, don't worry. The Universe has your back.

This Quiet Within

Come to the quiet,
leave your thoughts behind.
Rest and know, all is calm
in body, soul and mind.

There is no need to seek
or travel far and wide,
for quiet is within
where storms of life subside.

♥ ❤ ♥

FIRST CHAKRA
(Rooted and Grounded)

I'm stable, I'm rooted,
I'm connected to this earth,
no longer afloat
or questioning my worth.

If I were to choose
to fly above the birds,
I'll spread my wings
upon my terms.

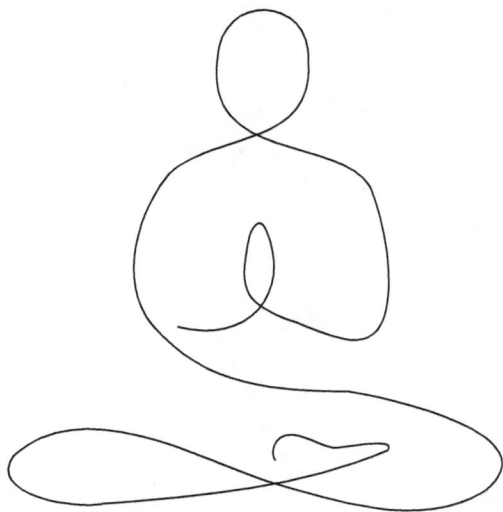

♥ ❧ ♥

THE TRYST
(Happily-Ever-After)

Trust the outcome
as if it doesn't matter.
Trust you will find
exactly what you're after.

A romantic rendezvous,
a walk beneath the clouds,
a shopping spree for rice and beans—
happily-ever-afters all around!

♥ ♥ ♥

How might you comfort yourself today?

Powered by Twiddle

Twiddle, twiddle,
I'm doing nothing but this.
These thumbs of mine
are a windmill of bliss.

I've been sitting a while
contemplating my navel,
and all I came up with
is this silly fable.

There's nothing better
for me, you see,
than to rest on my laurels,
so comfortably.

Twiddle, twiddle,
I'm doing nothing but this.
These thumbs of mine
are a windmill of bliss.

♥ 💕 ♥

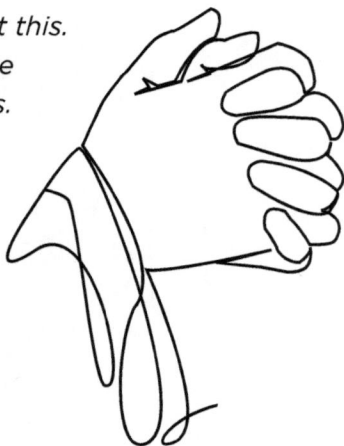

When you're done doing, all gets done.

The End

I've written about the birds,
the trees and peace.
I penned my thoughts
'til everything's released.

What do you say
when the words are spent?
How do you feel
when they're a forgotten event?

I've sat in stillness and contemplated,
meditated and visualized beyond satiated.
I've walked for miles in someone's shoes,
made and broken many rules.

You may think this ditty is not so pretty
and comes from a place of sadness.
Yet within this space, is my solace and grace—
in doing nothing, all's done through gladness.

♥ ♥ ♥

To Know and Be Known

Lately I have come to know God
as God knows me:
to enjoy and be enjoyed.

Lately I have come to know God
as God knows me:
to touch and be touched...
deeply, profoundly, fully.

With no beginning or finality,
embracing continuity and non-duality.
There's no start or end to us,
we continue even as dust turns to dust:
to know and be known.

Lately I have come to know God
as God knows me.

Resources
Feelings

Pleasant (expansion)

CALM
relaxation	grounded
serene	centered
tranquil	trusting
peaceful	relief
quiet	content
at ease	fulfilled
comfortable	satisfaction
at home	mellow

LIVELY
awake	vibrant
excitement	bliss
enthusiasm	ecstatic
eager	radiant
energetic	thrill
passionate	astonishment
alive	amazement
surprise	tingle

HAPPY
joy	delight
amusement	glad
animated	pleased

COMPASSION
tender	touched
warm	moved
open	affection
loving	friendly

CURIOUS
fascination	inspiration
interest	anticipation
involvement	wonder
engagement	

GRATEFUL
appreciation	thankful
openhearted	encouragement

CONFIDENT
empowerment
proud
hopeful
optimistic
strong

REFRESHMENT
rested
enlivened
restored
reactivation
clearheaded
exuberant

Unpleasant (constriction)

CONFUSION

torn
doubt
lost
hesitant
bafflement
perplexed
puzzled

BODY SENSATIONS

knot in the belly	shrink
lump in the throat	sick
inner rush	weak
disgust	empty
choking	shaky
breathless	dizzy
squeeze	foggy
trembling	cold

WORRY

anxious
edgy
unquiet
concern
stress/tense
nervous

ANNOYANCE

irritation
frustration
exasperation
impatient

FEAR

afraid
scared
suspicion
panic
paralyzed
terror
apprehension

SAD

heavy heart	hopeless
nostalgic	helpless
melancholy	gloomy
disappointment	down
discouragement	longing
depression	despair

ANGER

upset
furious
rage
resentful

FATIGUE

overwhelm
burn-out
exhaustion
sleepy
tired

PAIN

guilt	heartbreak
hurt	miserable
lonely	devastation
grief	regret
agony	remorseful
suffer	turmoil

HATE

hostile
aversion
bitter
disgust
contempt
dislike

VULNERABLE

fragile
insecure
reservation
sensitive

AGITATION

uncertain	alert
troubled	restless
unsettled	shock
cranky	uncomfortable
disquiet	uneasy

BOREDOM

apathetic
numb
far
withdrawn
disengaged

JEALOUS

envious

SHAME

embarrassment   shy

Universal Needs

PHYSICAL WELL-BEING

air
nourishment (food, water)
light
warmth
rest/ sleep
movement / physical
exercise
health
touch
sexual expression
shelter / security / safety /
emotional safety /
protection from pain /
protection / preservation
comfort

HARMONY

peace
beauty
calm / equanimity /
relaxation / tranquility
ease
order
coherence / congruence
sustainability
stability/ balance
communion / wholeness
completion / digestion /
integration
predictability/ familiarity
equality / justice / fairness

CONNECTION

love / self-love
care / self-care
belonging
closeness / intimacy
empathy / compassion
appreciation / gratitude
acceptance
recognition
reassurance
affection
attention
openness
trust
communication
sharing / exchange
giving / receiving
tenderness / softness
sensitivity / kindness
respect
seeing (see & be seen)
hearing (hear & be heard)
understanding (understand
& be understood)
consideration / inclusion /
that my needs matter /
participation
support/ help / nurturance
cooperation / collaboration
community / fellowship /
companionship / partnership
mutuality / reciprocity
consistency / continuity

MEANING

contribution / enrich life
presence / centeredness
self-connection
hope / vision / dream / faith
clarity / focus / concentration
to know (be in reality)
learning
awareness / consciousness
inspiration / creativity
challenge / stimulation
growth / evolution/ progress
expansion
exploration / development
power / (inner) strength /
empowerment
competence / capacity
self-value / self-confidence /
self-esteem / dignity/
efficacy / effectiveness
to matter / take part in /
have my place in the world
spirituality / purpose
liberation / transformation
interdependence
simplicity
celebration / mourning

FREEDOM

choice / acting out of my
own spirituality
autonomy
independence
space / time

HONESTY

authenticity
(self) expression
integrity
transparency
realness / truth

PLAY

liveliness / alive / vitality
flow
passion
spontaneity
fun
humor / laugh / lightness
discovery / adventure
variety / diversity
renewal / refreshment

Acknowledgements

I'm so grateful for the leading men in my life: Paul Anthony, my love for you is weaved throughout this book. Much gratitude also to David S, Michael S, Daniel P, Clayton–there's a poem written about each of you.

Always my guiding beacon and consistent cheerleader, huge thanks to my mother Malka for being there for me no matter what. A very special thanks to my brother Clive—you are the role model of a truly great man. My love and gratitude to my five children: Shayna, Jade, RaeAnne, Benjamin, Leeyah, and my grandson Coleton; I've learned a lot through our ups and downs.

Much appreciation to my dear friends, who love me and have served as delightful catalysts: Tracey, Mary L, Marilyn B, Greg S, Robin B, Sita, Chuck K, Joel, Pablo L, Kevin D, Dave M and Michael V. I also want to thank my dear adopted family Ingrid and Jeff.

This book wouldn't be the same without the indispensable help from my editors Lilly and Lahna. Many thanks also to my talented illustrator Cindy Blaser.

I am grateful to those of you who are choosing to read my book; thank you for having faith in me. Throughout my life, countless people have come and gone. You have all inspired me and helped me grow.

About the Author

After 15 years of chronic pain, heartbreak and depression, Shira Bliss has overcome multiple challenges and is living her best life. Born and raised in the United Kingdom in 1959, she has gleaned decades of wisdom to impart.

Shira helps bring sanctity to domestic violence survivors through relationship coaching and international workshops. She is a certified reiki practitioner and herbalist. Shira home birthed and home educated her five (now grown) children.

Known as the "Singing Poetess" she conducts sound healings to tune up the entire body's energy systems. When Ms. Bliss isn't planning tasty adventures for her San Diego Beer, Wine & Spirits Tours' guests, she can be found in her kitchen dancing and cooking or sitting quietly in nature.

Shira currently resides in her 250 sq. ft. tiny home in rural San Diego, CA.

Alphabetical Index by Title

Acting Like My Lover.................................10
À la carte.................................70
a moment in time.................................138
A Pleasant Pause.................................178
Arms Open Wide.................................197
Arrived.................................196
Assembled.................................194
A to B.................................171
Balancing Act.................................82
Becoming Friends.................................19
Be True to You.................................186
Bit By Bit (One Bite at a Time).................................140
Brass Ring.................................12
Calm Rapids.................................117
Carpe Diem.................................124
Catharsis.................................62
Celebrate You.................................123
Cherished.................................204
Choose You! (The Perfect Date).................................192
Comfort Or Pain?.................................26
Counterpoise (Tea and Sympathy).................................104
cozy and poetry.................................193
Damage and Reparation.................................146
Damn Good.................................145
Dilly-Dally.................................135
Directions.................................102
Do Unto Others.................................93
Easy (Breakfast in Bed).................................174
Easy Peasy (Shine On).................................77

Ebb & Flow 45
Ego She Go.. 78
Ego Speaks.. 34
Embraced.. 56
embracing my age................................. 167
Enchanté.. 166
Face Value.. 76
Fails With Flying Colors......................... 114
First Chakra (Rooted and Grounded)...... 214
First Kiss 160
Flow... 152
Fortified 13
Found Treasure 66
Fresh Eyes.. 190
Full Color 207
full days... 172
Get Lost! 119
Giggles & Guffaws................................. 86
Goldilocks 139
Graceful.. 20
Groovy Baby 73
Grow Up!... 39
Happy To Be... 183
Heart's Song 212
Hey You... 16
Hobnob With Me 81
Hunky-Dory 177
Hurry Slowly.. 99
I Am Love 173
I Am That... 59
If The Glove Fits...................................... 6

Innie Outie 170

I Ride on Your Words.............................. 159

Is There Anyone Out There? 33

It Is Enough 127

I've Got You 203

Kindling (Earth Angel) 115

Kinship.. 156

Kismet..209

K.I.S.S. (Keep It Simple Sweetie)........................ 75

Laissez-Faire 118

Let Go..121

let go even more 122

let it go..30

Let It Out..46

let me out.. 32

Let Them Be..176

Loosey-Goosey 90

Love Affairs 185

Love Makes the World Go 'Round 184

Love Song (To The Beloved Within)................ 142

Loving What Is 132

Mainstay..108

Make Your Mark 92

Many Paths — Same Sky 105

mindless.. 79

Mindless Too..80

Momentum.. 95

Moonlight Kisses 129

More 97

Much Ado About Nothing 67

My Companions (Sit Inside Your Being) 103

My Perfect Love 188

My World 64

Near & Far 195

Nichey Glitchy 136

Nonsense (The Place to Be) 128

Non-Toxic 98

No Place Like Home (Lush and Lively)...........144

No Sweeter Sound...................................147

No Vex Flex 87

No Waste.. 47

Nowhere Land 211

Of Love and War (Coming Home)......................111

Oneness 206

One Step at a Time.................................58

Operation Peace......................................50

Opportunities Knock (Hard!)...............36

Organic.. 168

Pain & Rebirth... 21

Parched...18

Passion Fruit (The Juice of Life) 63

Patience 110

peachy..182

Perfectly Imperfect 181

Pizza Delivery 71

Posthaste... 9

Powered by Twiddle................................216

Pure Gold 153

Quiet and Space....................................180

Richter Scale..2

Rise Above..100

Rise and Fall.. 27

Sacred Geometry 53
Sailing 143
sanity 72
Sans Souci 125
Self-Absorbed or Self-Love 101
Self-Care 29
Selfishly Giving 208
Self-Talk 210
Seven Days (One Weak) 31
Silence is Golden 88
Sit With Me (Lullaby of Friday) 205
Skin and Funny Bones 25
Slow Down 35
Soliloquy 154
speechless 161
Spot-On! 164
Stalemate 61
"Stand At Ease" 133
Static Quo 3
Step Inside (A Thousand Kisses) 155
Sticks and Stones 137
Success 60
Sweet Caramel 55
The City of Wonder 120
The Designer 54
The Diamond I am Today 44
The End 217
The Forest of Knowing 165
The Future of Now 134
The Gentle Gardener 106
the genuine article 24

The Gift 74

The Perfect Outfit 91

The Performance 37

The Portal 51

The Queen's Road 40

The "Right" Path (The Way) 112

The Same 5

The Sense of Bliss 162

The Tapestry of Life 89

The Tryst (Happily-Ever-After) 215

The Voices in My Head 109

The Warmth of You 158

The Way of Flow 85

The Whole Gamut 148

This Love Within 150

This Quiet Within 213

Timeless 191

To Err is Human 94

To Know and Be Known 218

Topsy-Turvy 107

True Love 202

Twenty-twenty 116

Unattached 84

unfettered 57

Unity 157

Unparalleled 200

Upside-Down 49

warm and golden 201

We Are Home 198

Weather Report: Calm with Showers
of Bliss 179

What If 96

wheat and chaff 126

Where Are My Marbles? 48

Where Are You? 8

Wherein I Wander 28

Who Am I? 149

Why Fight? 68

Why Wait? 69

Windows of the Heart 52

Winds of Change (Reassurance on a
Blustery Day) 175

wish upon a flower 38

Wistful 4

Within Your Smile (Daddy's Home) 42

Wriggly 14

yin and yang..113

You are Ideal 187